# The Serpent and the Sparrow

A Young Woman Chooses to Follow God . . .

Then Gets Brain Cancer

By
Christy Wilson

*All profits from the sale of this book go to*
*Consider the Sparrow*

# Table of Contents

This is a true story.
Some names and details have been changed.

"By faith Moses…endured, as seeing him who is invisible."
Hebrews 11:27

# The Serpent Takes Shape

*For whatever reason, I got really excited about your adventures today...I have no idea where you are at in life and what you are going through, but I do know that God is passionately pursuing you... whether you feel it or not, whether you believe it or not, whether you feel surrounded by Him or a million miles away, God wants your heart.*

*Love,*

*Christina*

If he listened carefully, he could hear the walls cry out. Moses stood, eyes closed, before a stack of bricks layered with the dried blood and tears of God's chosen people. He lifted a shaky hand and placed it on the wall's rough surface, feeling in its coarse texture the harsh existence of his people. He had spent the last forty years trying to forget about the cruelty that he now touched. But God had called him back here: to see the oppression....and to be the instrument of God's deliverance from it.

*I will be with you Moses.*
*I know Lord. I know.*

7

But Moses felt very alone in the shade of his people's torment.

"Moses?"

Startled, Moses lowered his hand and opened his eyes. His brother Aaron was staring at him.

"You ready?"

Moses' feet were sliding on a film of sweat in his sandals; his hands were fisted into bony knots. Behind the shield of his robes, his kneecaps quivered.

"Yes," Moses mumbled.

"Let's go then."

Moses watched Aaron's tall frame approach the gaping mouth of the brick building and disappear into its darkness. Moses stepped forward slowly, studying the gold lining that shimmered along the frame of the doorway. He reached a hand to touch a lip of gold that seemed to be dripping down the door frame. He quickly pulled his hand away. Egypt salivated...for him.

Moses took a deep breath and closed his eyes. *Okay, Lord. Okay. You are enough for me. I will enter the shadow of Death if You will go with me.*

*I am with you Moses.*

He stepped through the doorway into a darkness heavy with oppression. A short passageway extended before him, illuminated only by rows of torches along the walls.

At the end of the hall, a line of sentinels halted them at black wood double doors.

Aaron announced who they were and why they were there. A ripple of remarks passed through the contingent. One of the guards circled around them, staring particularly hard into Moses' eyes. Moses stared back, surprised that his shaking kneecaps blurred his sight. Then the guard grunted, turned and disappeared through a small door to the left.

Wordlessly, the Egyptians glowered at the two brothers. Moses stood behind Aaron, shifting from one slimy-bottomed foot to the other. He tried to ease his nerves by concentrating on the happy reunion he had shared with his people the night before.

When he had begun this journey back to Egypt he was unsure if any Hebrews would even still be alive in his childhood land. Happily, he found that they not only lived, they thrived. Then he was fearful of how they would receive him. But after he and Aaron had performed the Lord's signs and delivered the Lord's message, the people had accepted them. And hope had landed in Goshen again. Last night had been a glorious evening: a time of celebration, reunion, and renewed dreams.

Moses almost smiled as he relived the happy evening.

With a grinding rumble, the double doors in the shady hallway opened. Light flooded the passageway, momentarily blinding Moses. He shielded his eyes.

Two guards stepped into position beside them. Moses could feel along the left side of his body the heat of the guard.

They walked into the heart of Egypt.

Moses' eyes quickly scanned the room. It was massive, hoarding all the wealth and prestige you would expect to find at the top of the human power chain. Light poured through gold-plated archways recessed in the painted ceiling. Inscriptions to the gods outlined the walls, where battle scenes were drawn in sequential hieroglyphics. Thick marble columns formed incisors, symmetrically rowed from one end of the room to the other. Clumps of mats and recliners sat in corners and around tables of food. Scented men and painted women grouped in active hives. A lion slept in the far corner of the room, a thick chain holding it to the wall.

Moses walked behind Aaron along a trail of basalt stones set into the marble floor. The path led them through the columns, past the partiers, by the opulence. They were drawn forward by the dark stones…indeed, everything in the room seemed to push them in one direction; all things deferential to the figure they now approached.

A marble platform rose before them, furnished only with a golden throne. A figure in white was laid out in boredom. On either side of the platform stood statues of a serpent, mid-strike. Moses found himself staring at the two statues. When he finally pulled his eyes away, his gaze fell to the real live Serpent of Egypt.

Pharaoh's eyes bored into him. Moses' heart strained to beat.

The two guards stopped, waiting to be acknowledged.

Pharaoh flicked his hand.

One of the guards announced, "Aaron and Moses, sons of Amram. Hebrews."

Their introduction caused the entire room to take a deep indignant breath, seeming to collect all oxygen and leave nothing but a stifling emptiness. Moses' lungs pushed against his chest, seeking clear air.

Aaron didn't hesitate.

"Pharaoh! God, the God of Israel, says, 'Free my people so that they can hold a festival for me in the wilderness.'"

Pharaoh leaned forward in his chair, coiled. He glared at the two brothers. "I don't know this god!"

Moses had expected Pharaoh to decline. God as much as told him this would happen.

Aaron tried again. "The God of Israel has met with us. Let His people take a three-day journey into the wilderness so we can worship Him, or else He will strike us."

Pharaoh slowly rose. "Why in the entire kingdom of Egypt would you ask that your people be given a holiday? Look at all these people bumming around me..." Pharaoh indicated with a wave of his hand the slaves waving his feathered fans and holding his pets, "And now you want me to reward them with time off?"

Pharaoh scanned the room again. "No!" he shouted. "They'll go back to work! They are lazy, and that is why they are crying out, 'Let us go and sacrifice to our God.' Make the work harder for them so that they keep working and stop listening to lies."

Moses looked out the corner of his eye to see Aaron stiffen.

Pharaoh commanded his henchmen to deliver new orders to the Hebrew foremen that they were henceforth to gather their own straw for bricks... while still making the same amount each day. Without even looking back at Moses and Aaron, Pharaoh went back to his throne, sat down and began to eat the food his servants placed before him.

And that was that.

With a quick escort down another dark hall, Moses and Aaron were expelled out the tail end of the monster's lair. Moses breathed deeply once outside.

They trudged silently back to Goshen, hearts heavy.

As they entered the boundaries of the Hebrew settlement, they could tell that word of Pharaoh's new decrees had beaten them there. Hostile stares greeted them. Mothers beckoned to their children, pulling them out of the path of destruction Moses and Aaron seemed to leave in their wake. Men crossed their arms and formed a path through which the brothers had to walk.

Someone called out:

"May the Lord look upon you and judge you!"

Another voice agreed: "Yeah! You've made us a stench to

Pharaoh and his officials and have put a sword in their hand to kill us."

Moses hung his head.

He had left behind a great life in Midian to come here and deliver the Hebrews, and here he was walking a gauntlet of shame in Goshen. Pharaoh's stubbornness had turned the hearts of Moses' own people against him. It was with good reason that some people referred to the Pharaoh as the Serpent of Egypt. His conniving trickery had successfully halted a Hebrew revival before it had even begun. Moses had never expected an easy journey. But this serpent threatened to suck the hope right out of his soul.

Moses walked alongside his brother Aaron. In his hand he held the staff of the Lord. But he still had many questions about where that staff would lead him.

# August 29<sup>th</sup>, 2007

It was a Wednesday.

Christina was preparing for her last client at the chiropractor's office. Spreading the last wrinkle out of the sheet on the massage table, she hit start on the CD player and walked out of her room. The lobby was small and quiet. Brown carpet ran the length of the room, casting that new-carpet-smell into the air. Metal chairs with blue cushions lined the three walls that faced the receptionist's desk. A man sat in one of the chairs flipping through a magazine, tapping his feet.

"Rick?" she said questioningly.

The man looked up with a small smile. Tossing his magazine, he grabbed the bag at his feet and approached her.

"Hi, I'm Christina."

He was handsome. "Nice to meet you," he said. The black hat on his head failed to contain a mess of wavy brown hair. His skin glistened, like he had just finished a game of tennis.

Christina made sure to grip his hand hard so he would know she could handle his tensions.

In the massage room, she let Rick describe his pain. As she listened, she felt a familiar pinch creeping up her neck from her shoulders.

*Oh no Lord. Not now. I'm almost done Lord. Just another hour.*

While Rick undressed, Christina walked to the lobby where Elda sat at the desk, her fingers beating rhythms on the keyboard.

"Almost done?" Elda asked cheerily.

"Yeah." Christina rocked her head back and forth a couple times, stretching her neck muscles. The pinch ebbed a little.

*One more hour, Lord. I just need the strength for one more hour.*

These prayers were frequent on Christina's workdays. She'd feel a headache coming on, pray for strength and press on, sometimes through excruciating pain. Such had been the last several months for her.

"Got any plans for the evening?" Elda asked.

"Oh yeah. BIG plans. After youth group, I'm planning on sitting on my couch at home. It's a big couch...huge." Christina had her arms extended straight out to her sides, as one telling a fishing tale. "Come over some time and I'll show you how huge it is. Then you'll have big plans too."

Elda laughed.

Christina checked the clock. Two minutes was usually enough time for the client to properly cover. She knocked on the door. At the muffled "Yeah," she opened the door and quietly entered. The music was soft and lilting, sending gentle waves of sound throughout the room. The room was peaceful. She hoped Rick was feeling it. Today she was feeling it. She prayed for God's guidance on this man's body.

She gently applied effleurage strokes down the muscles along his spine. Her palms rode firmly down his back, acquainting her hands to his skin, and vice versa. She gradually applied more pressure as she tracked along the tough fibers in his trapezius, the broad muscle spanning the shoulders. There was tension there. There was always tension in the trapezius. It's the muscle that carries all the modern day problems of almost every client she touched. As she pressed towards Rick's shoulders, she could feel her own trapezius tighten.

She lifted her head to give her neck a break. Her eyes traveled along the wall of her room. A diagram of the human muscular system was right in front of her. Next to it was the coat rack where Rick's hat hung. It had some white lettering on its front. Christina squinted to read the words. She squinted harder. The letters weren't materializing for her. She thought she saw an A, but she couldn't be sure. It was like there was a word there, with another overlaying it.

Her hands had traveled up into the man's hair. She looked down on his bare back, so clear to her. She looked back at the hat, so not clear. She shook her head, and focused on her work, a new pinch materializing in her trapezius.

After the hour was up, Christina said farewell to Rick and went back to strip the table. At her doorway she paused, looking to the end of the hallway where an eye chart hung. The big E stared her down as if challenging her. Christina turned to face the chart, her arms still full of sheets.

E.

F, P.

T, O, Z.

Christina squinted. "Hey Elda?"

"Yes?"

"Could you come here real quick?"

Slide, shuffle. Elda was at her side. "You okay?"

"Well, I think so. Can you read the eye chart down there?"

Elda looked down the hall, pursing her lips. "Um, let's see: E, F, P, T, O, Z, L, P, E, D, P, E, C, F, D…how far down do you want me to go?"

"Clearly, you can read it just fine."

"It gets a little fuzzy in that second section. Is that a D, E, E…uh?…B?" Elda stopped and chuckled. "I think I'm just guessing now."

Christina glared down the hall again at the white rectangle with the clear E. "Well, I can't read past the third line."

"No!"

"Yeah. I'm totally serious. It's weird. I just looked down the hall, and found myself …illiterate, or something."

"Strange."

"Yeah, and when I was massaging that last guy, I looked at his hat on the wall, and I couldn't read the words on it. I still don't know what it said."

"Strange," Elda said again.

Christina took the sheets to the back room for washing. Back in the lobby, she asked, "Can a person's eyes just go funky all of a sudden?"

"I…don't think so," Elda said hesitantly.

Christina looked out the lobby's window to the street sign on the stoplight. "Can you read the street name on that sign out there? On the stoplight?"

Elda searched through the window. "You mean Grant Street? Yeah, I can read that."

Christina shrugged her shoulders. "I can't!"

"Is it blurry?"

"No. Not really. It's just like not focused…if I close one eye it's a little better…but..."

"That's strange Christina."

"I know. Maybe I need glasses."

"Maybe you do. You would look cute with glasses."

"Yeah…I'd look sooooo smart," Christina quipped. She pressed her finger up the ridge of her nose to resituate hypothetical specs. She puckered her lips like a British nanny.

Elda smiled. "Yeah, you'd look good."

"Oh Elda," Christina pushed up her fake glasses one more time, "You're the best!"

"Oh, come now..." Elda drawled, clearly pleased.

"You are!" Christina trilled. She turned the lights off in her room, threw her purse over her shoulder, and headed for the door. Elda gave Christina a sweet, everyday 'farewell,' as if this were an everyday.

· · · · · · · · ·

Christina drove home cautiously. While considering the clarity, or lack thereof, of her vision, she constantly monitored her every move: the turn of the steering wheel, the presence of every car and pedestrian around her... just in case. If awareness makes a cautious driver, Christina was a mobile air bag.

Her mind raced with questions. What is going on Lord? Am I crazy? Do I suddenly need glasses at 25-years-old? Is the tension in my neck affecting my sight? Am I going blind?

The sense of panic rising in her belly moved up her chest, making her heart beat faster. She gripped the wheel more tightly.

*Will you follow Me?*

The words were audible to no one but Christina, but they were as clear as if someone sitting on the seat next to her had said them.

Christina took a deep breath. Am I following Jesus, or what?

"Yes!" she spoke aloud.

· · · · · · · · ·

That fall of 2007, she was 25.

Quite clearly, she was young.

Christina Ahmann had the look of a woman and a child at the same time. Her face had the bone structure of a movie star, but the boisterous smile and twinkling eyes of a kid who's just discovered a crab under a beach rock. She had a crescent of freckles extending from one cheek to the other. Her eyes were blue-colored frosting.

She was an introvert. She loved her solitude; but her love for people was deeper and more powerful. She wanted to know people. She cared, truly cared. The things that brought her to tears were the shared feelings of others' experiences: the pains and joys felt by those she loved. She was the type of person who would spelunk with you into the depths of your soul to shine a light upon your secrets, fears and loves.

But she loved to laugh too. And she loved to make people burst into a belly-laugh. Like yeast, she was a quiet person that, when placed in the right mix, bubbled over with effervescence. She was just as likely to hold your hand as you cried through a difficult situation, as she was to randomly give you a titty-twister just to hear you squeal. She liked to push the social envelope, drawing people into silly, sometimes awkward moments, to shine a light on her, and everyone else's common humanity.

This intimacy came easily between Christina and those with whom she was comfortable. But, when faced with a group of strangers, Christina would often find herself plagued by two of her closest childhood companions: shyness and timidity. And any group attention that centered on her...well, that would pretty much incapacitate her. She could be deeply transparent, but also protectively reserved.

This was the young woman who was about to stare into the face of a dangerous serpent.

. . . . . . . . .

That night, after hanging out with her youth group girls, Christina wound down in the suburban home she shared with her roommate, Linsey. The girls sat next to each other on the couch. Linsey was scanning the Web, her thick glasses perched on her nose like a happy thought. Christina was scanning the room, testing her vision on the items in the room. She studied the movies shelved underneath the TV. She couldn't read a single title. She looked at Linsey's purse, hanging on a hook next to the door. Metal clasps winked blurry reflections of light at her. She closed one eye. The shine seemed to focus a bit more...just a bit. She closed the other eye. Yeah...maybe a smidge better.

Christina looked over at her best friend. "Don't," she said loudly.

"No, you don't," Linsey said loudly back, her eyes not leaving the computer screen.

This was their greeting, their way of getting each other's attention, their secret code of connection.

Linsey finished typing something and looked at her.

"Can a person's eyes just go funky all of a sudden?" Christina asked.

Looking at Christina through the strong prescription of her own glasses, Linsey's face scrunched. "I don't think so Teena. Why?"

"Oh, my eyes just seem to be having a little trouble today."

"Like what kind of trouble?"

"I don't know. Just trouble. I was giving this guy a massage and I looked at his hat hanging on the wall...he was wearing an Adidas sweatshirt, by the way..."

Linsey smiled. Her boyfriend worked for Adidas.

"Anyway, his hat was hanging on the wall, and it had letters on it...white letters on a black hat. I couldn't read the letters."

Linsey frowned. "Like, they were blurry?"

"No...I don't...just funky."

"That's weird."

"I know."

"Let's google it." Linsey pounded some keys on her computer. "Eyes go funky," she said.

Christina sat up, a smile on her face.

"'Do you mean funny?'" Linsey read from the screen. "No, I mean 'funky.' Ah, here we go. Funky makeup ideas. Funky eyeliners." Linsey laughed loudly, a clear, bell-like sound. "Does Teena need some funky eye shadow?"

"Yeah, for sure. It would go nicely with the rest of the makeup I wear." Christina flashed a hand over the bare skin of her face.

"Oh, hey! This person's talking about her kitten's eyes going funky," Linsey said. "Let's see....Oh, they go in opposite directions sometimes. Do yours do that?"

"Ooops, there they go again," Christina said, crossing her eyes. "I hate it when they do that."

"Oh, funky eyeglasses." Linsey clicked on the link. "Ooooh, maybe I should get some of these." She pointed with her finger at an image of purple eyeglasses with four concentric circles around each eyehole.

"Yuck."

"So you're saying I shouldn't get them?"

"How about those?" Christina pointed at a pair of pink glasses with the first eyehole cut in the shape of an 'I' and the second in the shape of a 'C.'

The girls practically knocked the computer off the couch with their laughter.

17

"All they need is a cut of a 'U' over the nose. 'I C U.'"

Linsey gripped the computer tightly as they laughed again.

"Oh man," they both sighed after the jolly peals died down.

"Okay, so clearly that wasn't helpful."

Christina sighed. "That's all right."

Linsey closed her laptop. "You should go to my eye doctor. She's really good."

"Yeah, maybe I will."

Linsey stretched her arms up to the ceiling.

"Could you....?" Christina let the question linger in the air, not wanting to ask it fully.

Linsey sighed. "All right. Lay down."

Christina lay back on the leather couch, her head aiming towards Linsey. Linsey's hands crawled under Christina's head, her fingers firmly planting at the base of her skull. Christina sighed as Linsey began to gently pull back on her head. The traction slightly eased some of the pressure on her neck and shoulders. It always helped...a little.

"Does it do anything for your eyesight?" Linsey asked.

Christina looked up at the black-rimmed light on the ceiling... both of them. "Nope."

"Hmm," Linsey said.

Christina tried to relax, tried to will away the pain that seemed to live in her neck and shoulders these days.

"Wanna watch a movie?" Linsey asked, her bright blue eyes perky and awake.

Christina sat up and looked at the clock. Eleven pm. This morning had been a headache morning. She had been awakened by a painful headache at 5:30 am and had not taken a nap all day. These were the days that felt like they would never end. "I can't Linsey. It's so late."

"It's not like we've never started a movie at eleven o'clock before," Linsey said, pulling out her 'convince, cajole, persuade' tone.

"Yeah, I know...but that was back in my younger days." Christina said with a smile. "You know...22-23."

"Younger, shmunger," Linsey said with a dismissive wave of her hand. Linsey's dog, Lucy, jumped up into Christina's lap. Lucy was a little brown and white terrier mutt with catawampus ears that couldn't agree on which direction they wanted to point: up, down, or sideways… so they both did their own thing, independent of the other. Right now, Lucy's left ear was straight out to the side, and her right ear rested down against her head. Christina rubbed Lucy's head.

"Dus da Teena think she's gettin' oooolllldddd?!!" Linsey burst out in The Voice. Lucy perked up as she always did when The Voice came out, both her ears now standing straight up. Linsey made The Voice by stretching her vocal chords until she sounded like a hyper robot addressing a small child. The Voice went back to the beginning of the girls' relationship, and it was as fresh and funny to them every time they did it as it had been the very moment they had first invented it.

"Yes she's gettin' soooo oooolllllddd!" Christina said, employing The Voice herself.

"What're we gonna do 'bout dat oooollllllddddd Teeena?" Linsey asked Lucy.

Lucy barked at being addressed in such a way. The girls laughed, endlessly amused by themselves.

Not much later, Christina fell asleep with the number of Linsey's eye doctor on a piece of paper at her desk, and thoughts of what God had in store for her swirling in her mind.

· · · · · · · · ·

What's a good friend?

A warm, hearty soup.

What's a good friend to a 25-year-old, just starting a career in a new town?

Prime rib.

What's a best friend to a 25-year-old, single girl, confronting life and adult responsibilities, trying to serve the Lord the best she can?

Water.

Vital.

Christina and Linsey together were like a Jacuzzi tub: they were a well of warmth, and depth; all just the push of a button away from eruptions of loud, raucous giggles and commotion. Conversations didn't just flow between them; they jetted back and forth on waves of common humor and decades-old history.

．．．．．．．．．

A 5-year-old Christina sat inside, playing with her closest companions, shyness and timidity. Outside she could hear the sounds of her older brother Jesse playing with that neighbor girl again. Christina sat with her doll, trying to play tea party, but unable to concentrate past the laughter of the neighbor girl outside as she and Jesse gathered stones to decorate.

"Oooh! Look at this rock! Jesse! Look at this!" the neighbor girl was shouting.

"Yeah," Jesse said in his lackadaisical little boy way.

"This rock looks just like a banana! See! Do you see how it looks like a banana? I'm going to paint it yellow, and keep it forever."

"Whatcha doing Christina?" Christina looked up. Her mom stood in the kitchen doorway wiping her hands on a towel.

"Playing," Christina answered, trying not to miss any words from outside.

"You can go out there and play with them if you want to, you know," her mom gently said to her.

Christina shook her head, unwilling to leave her two companions.

"Okay," her mother said with a slightly sad shrug.

Christina listened some more. Things had gone quiet outside. Then suddenly...

"Jesse! You painted on MY rock! That was MY rock! Why did you do that? I was going to paint my rock. It was my favorite."

"I just grabbed one..."

"You grabbed MY rock! You painted it red! I was going to paint it yellow! Like a banana!"

"I'm sorry, I just..."

"No you're not! You did that on purpose! I don't ever want to play with you again... ever, ever, ever!"

"C'mon..."

"No! I won't play with you ever, ever again!"

Christina heard some rocks fall to the ground. Then little footsteps tromped around the house. She got up quickly from the couch and ran across the room to the window facing the street. The neighbor girl sat on the sidewalk, facing Christina's house, her head down on folded arms. Her shoulders went up and down quickly.

20

Christina watched her for a minute. Then she slowly got up from her chair, placed her doll down and, bringing her closest companions, walked outside.

The girl was sobbing... loudly! If Jesse was supposed to be responding to the tears of his playmate, he wasn't doing his job. So Christina walked slowly toward the scene of the noisy pity party, stopped across the street and sat down on the curb across the road from her.

The girl's eye peeked up from the crook of her elbow. She stopped sobbing at the sight of Christina. She had long brown hair and piercing blue mischievous eyes.

"Oh..."

Christina said nothing, just shyly flitted her eyes up to the girl and back to the ground.

The girl watched Christina a moment. Then she said, "You wanna play?"

Christina shrugged. "Sure."

"I'm Linsey."

"I'm Christina."

"I'm six."

"I'm five."

"Hey! Do you want to play a fun game!"

"Sure."

"Let's play detective!"

"Okay."

"We're called the Fox Club, and we have to solve mysteries."

"Okay."

"Okay, follow me."

"Okay."

• • • • • • • • •

And so began the friendship.

They were inseparable. In fact, when either girl got in trouble and had to suffer the consequences of their actions, their parents would ground them from each other.

"You cannot play with Linsey today."

"But Mom....!"

"You'll have to call Christina and cancel your afternoon together."

"Awww Mom...!"

Their families loved the relationship. Linsey was an only child and therefore her parents appreciated Linsey having a good playmate. And Christina's parents celebrated the friend that drew their daughter out of her shell.

Christina and Linsey grew up together. They attended the same private Christian school, spending every other year in the same classroom because grades were stacked together...1st and 2nd, 3rd and 4th, 5th and 6th.

Then, when Linsey was in 7th grade, her family bought a jewelry store in Sequim, the neighboring town, and moved away. When they reached high school, they both went to their respective town's schools. They got together occasionally, but not often.

Unbeknownst to them, they picked the same college after graduating one year apart. They remained friends, but their social lives were separate and they did not see much of each other.

When Christina graduated from Westmont in 2004, she decided to go to massage school in Portland. Knowing that Linsey had already settled there, she called her up.

"Hey, by any chance, do you need a roommate?"

"Actually, yeah!"

They had been living together ever since.

Christina was Mary to Linsey's Martha. Linsey was a go-getter, talented in many ways, friends with many people, unafraid of anything. Christina was the quiet one, inclined to sit and listen, follow and support, observe and absorb. They complemented one another perfectly. Together they waded through relationships, learned about finances, grew up and served the Lord. They were vital to one another... water.

. . . . . . . . .

The next day, Christina made a phone call.

"Mom?"

"Hi Christina. How's it going?"

"So...is it normal for vision to change suddenly?"

Pause. "What do you mean 'change suddenly'?"

"Well..." Christina laid out the scenario from the day before.

As Christina talked, JoDee Ahmann understood right away that things had been going on with her daughter of which she had not been privy to. Over the phone, Christina shared more than she ever had before about a year-long accumulation of symptoms and bodily frustrations.

At one point during Christina's explanations, she used the words 'double vision.' JoDee stopped her daughter mid-confession. "Christina! You hang up the phone and call your doctor right away."

"You think so?"

"Right now Christina!"

"Okay."

* * * * * * * *

Christina came from good stock. Doug and JoDee Ahmann raised their children in Port Angeles, Washington with loving, God-fearing hands. Christina's older brother, Jesse, treated her as all older brothers should: with a protective love, occasionally sprinkled with irritation.

Doug was an accountant and a father who made his kids feel adored. Always wearing a joyful smile and a servant's willingness, he cared for his family with diligence, and perseverance.

JoDee was a musician. Christina's childhood was filled with the vibrating strings of young violinists come to glean the wisdom of her mother's experienced artistry. Christina herself had knelt at the footstool of her mother's talent, taking lessons from her throughout her entire childhood.

With Christina and JoDee as violinists, and Jesse an accomplished cellist, the family was ¾ of a quartet waiting to happen. Recognizing this, Doug took his mathematical mind and a long-past experience as a musician, and shouldered the musical burden for his family's sake: he learned to play viola. The Ahmanns took their quartet into their church, playing for worship and occasional weddings.

Such was the camaraderie in Christina's family.

* * * * * * * *

After telling Christina to call the doctor, JoDee hung up and started to pray. At the words 'double vision,' JoDee's mind had immediately jumped to a possibility, a change of landscape for the Ahmann family. Later that day, she walked to her computer and typed in 'brain tumor.' She read through the list of symptoms, shaking her head at their familiarity: "debilitating morning headaches, neck problems, hearing issues, blurry vision."

23

That night, JoDee discussed the issue with Doug, who wasn't sure what to think.

The next morning, she took her Bible, her journal, and her fears and walked upstairs. A quiet room on the second floor was where she spent her time before the Almighty. She sat down in a blue suede chair listening to the sound of chirping birds outside.

That morning, she systematically picked out each and every possibility for the future of her daughter, studied it, cried over it, and laid it at the foot of the Throne.

"It could be nothing...a false alarm...

"I will follow You Lord.

"It could be a benign growth in her head....

"I will follow You Lord."

She went through each scenario, from false alarm, to the death of her daughter. And she let each one go, professing her devotion to God, and holding tightly to the promise of Isaiah 40:

"He speaks tenderly to those with young."

• • • • • • • • •

Christina called JoDee back on Friday to tell her the doctor would see her the next Tuesday. JoDee cancelled her life, told Doug her plans and made preparations for the 4 ½ hour drive to Portland.

• • • • • • • • •

"Christina!"

The ball hit Christina's hands at the same time as Mandy's warning. Christina gripped the leather ball as Linsey charged toward her.

Before vaulting the basketball at the hoop 5 feet away, Christina shouted, "Fifty- fifty chance I make it in the right basket." She launched it right at the middle of the image her eyes saw.

The ball banked off the backboard directly into Linsey's hand. She and Robbie cheered their rebound.

"I think you aimed at the wrong hoop," Mandy said with a playful shove.

Christina shoved Mandy back and got into a defensive position, ignoring the fierce, pounding pain in her head.

Robbie was Linsey's boyfriend; a fun-loving, creative mind-in-shoes. Mandy was a friend from Christina's childhood; a friend 20-

24

years strong. She was in Portland for a visit; a visit planned before Christina's eyes had funktified. The teams were aligned with two real basketball players, Mandy and Robbie, on opposite teams, each handicapped by a teammate with poor vision, Christina and Linsey respectively. For the most part, those two ladies threw their bodies around, creating presence on the court with their noise and movements, while Mandy and Robbie took each other's skills to task. Occasionally Christina or Linsey would be used as a backboard or a distraction.

It was Sunday. Here she was, shooting hoops with three of her favorite people on earth, as if life was normal. But she could sense an approaching storm. Things were about to change.

And though Christina's vision was currently marred, one thing was very clear: God was in charge. Life was full of curveballs, obstacles, and challenges…she had faced down many over the last few months. And always, God had shown Himself to be enough. There was infinite peace in that truth.

Robbie had the ball, Mandy defending him, her body crouched low to the ground, eyes fixed on Robbie's core.

Christina's body was pressed up against Linsey's who was more interested in cheering on Robbie's moves than in getting open for him. She made a half-hearted attempt to cut to the right side of her teammate. Christina followed close behind, wrapping her long slender arms around her roommate. Linsey brought her arms down tightly over Christina's so that their arms were intertwined. They laughed and slapped at each other. Robbie made a quick fake to the left, then charged toward the twister pose of Linsey and Christina. Mandy rammed into the two girls, one of her arms snagging underneath Christina's armpit. Robbie sauntered alone to the hoop where he effortlessly laid the ball against the backboard and through the basket. Mandy groaned. Christina grinned sheepishly. Linsey cheered loudly in both their ears.

Robbie high-fived Linsey, "Thanks for the screen."

"Screen? What's that?"

At that moment, Christina's cell phone rang loudly from the ground next to the court.

"That's probably my mom…she must be here."

"Tell her to come over here. We have to finish this game," Robbie said, his eyes on Mandy.

A few minutes later, the approach of a pretty woman with dark brown shoulder-length hair brought the game to a close and Christina led the way to greet her mom.

The foursome circled JoDee in a flurry of sweaty, breathy bodies. Christina hugged her mother tightly.

JoDee pulled away and studied Christina, noting her flushed cheeks, her heaving chest. Her newly educated mind was on the lookout for signs, symptoms, anything that might give cause for alarm...and she was quite alarmed by Christina's physically strained state. How could she be out shooting hoops, raising her blood pressure, pushing her heart and lungs to the limit, when there were so many possible ailments that could be ravaging her body at that very moment?

Exercising enormous self-control, JoDee kept a calm demeanor as she greeted her daughter and friends. "What are you guys doing?"

"Shooting a few hoops," Linsey answered.

"Schooling these two," Robbie suggested.

Christina put her arm around her mother. Addressing Robbie's boast, she said, "Well, it's hard to play basketball when there's two of everything!"

JoDee shook her head at the joke.

In a relationship between a mother and her adult daughter, what dictates the emotional space that will hold a mother's worries? Does a mother share the burden of her fears for her children with those very children? Can a child even comprehend the searing pain a mother feels when the torch of her motherly love catches sight of a worldly, dangerous shadow around her children?

While these questions were present in the moment, they did not create a space between mother and daughter that day, or ever. JoDee was there. Christina was there. And God was there. That was enough.

. . . . . . . . .

That afternoon, mother and daughter took a walk.

Portland was a city very much alive. It bustled with industry, creativity, progress and family. The neighborhood where Christina shared a house with Linsey was within the city limits, but with the cozy feel of a small suburban community. The houses all shared a similar look, products of a development in the seventies. The lots were evenly spaced apart from one another, with well-kept lawns and bushy rhododendrons forming lively boundaries: short enough to visit over, tall enough to define spaces. As fall approached, the cycle of fecundity and decay was completing its turn among the leaves of the thirty-year-old oak trees that lined the streets. The brushstroke of the Lord was beginning to leave swaths of yellow and orange among the branches. In about a month's time, those colorful leaves would fall from their posts, collecting in piles three feet high along the streets, like bumpers at a bowling alley.

Christina waved at a neighbor out watering her dahlias.

JoDee smiled at the neighbor. Then she cleared her throat and said, "So…"

"So…" Christina responded.

"Have you thought about the possibility…" pause "…that this could be a brain tumor?"

Christina pursed her lips, looked at her mother and said, "Yeah."

JoDee's jaw dropped and she grabbed Christina's arm. "What?!"

Christina smiled sheepishly.

"If you've thought about this, even fathomed the possibility that you might have a brain tumor, why is this the first time I've heard anything about it?"

"I don't know. It's not like I've been sitting around in my room and crying about some darn tumor I might have."

"But, even if you've had a fleeting thought, that's a heavy thing to carry alone Christina!" JoDee continued to stare at Christina with shock. "Why would you not talk to someone about it? Did you mention that thought to Linsey?"

"No."

"Christina…"

"Mom, really, I've been living with these ailments for so long now…" Christina paused, thinking back, "…really, about a year… and I always felt so lame because of them…I don't know… I just sort of stopped talking about them. I didn't want to complain, or dwell on them. Linsey has had to deal with enough of my problems this year as it is."

"And you didn't want to be a burden?" JoDee said, finishing Christina's unspoken creed.

"Yeah, I guess so."

"And clearly, you haven't been very forthcoming about your physical condition with us either. I called Linsey after we talked last

27

Friday and asked her how often you've been having these headaches, when, and how long they last. She told me more than you have."

"I know. I'm sorry," Christina said. She remained reticent about her trials so as not to burden those she loved. Now she wondered if that had been the right decision.

"It just breaks my heart to think of you going through something all alone Christina."

"I know."

"Well," JoDee said, moving away from the issue, "there needs to be an MRI. I've heard stories of doctors being hesitant to order them, when they clearly should. I'm here to make sure they order one."

Christina nodded, knowing that wasn't the only reason her mom was there.

"You tell 'em mom."

They walked quietly a moment. A neighbor was out clipping dahlias. She waved at them. Christina waved back. Cars passed occasionally, sending gentle breezes over the ladies.

"You know Mom, I'm just ready. I'm ready to find out whatever has been causing all this pain in my life and to move forward."

JoDee nodded.

Christina turned the tables. "Are you ready? For...whatever?"

JoDee looked into her eyes and said, "Yes. I've had my conversation with God. I'm ready."

Christina looked sideways at her mom searching for hidden pain. Christina didn't want to see that pain; it would crush her to see her mom hurting because of her. She truly hoped JoDee's courageous demeanor and answers were genuine.

*Please Lord, let this be nothing, she prayed, for my parents' sake.*

"Wanna have another conversation with God?"

And mother and daughter prayed.

• • • • • • • •

That night, Christina, Mandy and Linsey went to dinner with JoDee. Christina drove, JoDee sitting shotgun. The sky had clouded over and raindrops were pelting the windshield. The wipers swished gently back and forth, clearing the line of sight repeatedly. Christina squinted her eyes at the road before her. If only she had wipers that could clear her vision so seamlessly.

She had reached the restaurant and needed to make a left-hand turn into the busy traffic of downtown Portland. She sat in the lane, blinker on, wipers swishing. A collection of bright lights were pointed in her direction, slowly growing in size until a car would appear and pass her by on the left. There was a steady stream of these lights, like a mob of people wielding magna flashlights coming directly at her. Until the shape of the car would form in the gray wetness before her, Christina could not tell how far away it was.

JoDee looked over at her daughter, seeing her stare intently at the oncoming traffic. Several openings in the cars passed and still, Christina did not turn.

A car horn sounded.

Christina had no idea if they were honking at her, but she began to sweat.

"Mom," she said, her eyes not leaving the road, "how far away are those cars?"

"You can't tell?" Linsey asked incredulously.

"Oh great! We've got the blurry-eyed girl driving," Mandy joked.

JoDee stared at her daughter, shocked.

"Well..." Christina said hesitantly, "it's hard...with the rain...and all the lights."

"Christina, I will tell you when to turn, okay?" JoDee said authoritatively.

Ten seconds later, JoDee said, "Now!"

Christina watched a clump of flashlights descending upon her, but she pressed firmly on the gas pedal and turned the wheel rapidly. The car bumped over the sidewalk ramp. Christina pulled into a parking spot, set the brake and took a deep breath. She released her tight grip on the steering wheel.

Turning to her wide-eyed passengers, Christina said, "Sorry 'bout scaring you."

Her friends smiled at her. JoDee said, "I'll drive home."

Three heads nodded.

They piled out of the car, and enjoyed a meal together. JoDee watched her daughter as they ate.

· · · · · · · ·

Dr. Suzanne Jacobsen was a well known family physician in

Portland. Before she had ever become a patient of Dr. Jacobsen's, Christina had heard her name several times from clients at her old physical therapy clinic.

Christina was sheepish when Dr. Jacobsen opened the door to the examination room. "Hello again, Christina."

"Hi," Christina said. "This is my mom JoDee."

Dr. Jacobsen shook JoDee's hand.

"So, it sounds like more than just your ear is bothering you," Dr. Jacobsen said, scanning the medical chart in her hand.

Hence Christina's sheepishness. Not three weeks earlier, Christina had sat in this very clinic, talking with this very woman about one thing...just one thing. She had outlined a discomfort in her ear for Dr. Jacobsen, wondering why she could distinctly hear her heartbeat in her right ear. Dr. Jacobsen had called it allergies, given her a prescription and sent her on her way.

Now Christina was back with the full story...the one about months of headaches, neck tension, nausea and vomiting, fatigue and now, double vision.

"You said nothing about any of this when you were in a couple weeks ago!" Dr. Jacobsen seemed a little upset. Her soft kind eyes flashed with intensity behind her glasses. Wisps of her graying blonde hair waved back and forth, like fingers wagging at a naughty child.

"I know, I know," Christina said shaking her head. "I want you to know, I don't blame you at all for not knowing something else could be wrong...I did not tell you all I was experiencing."

"No you did not." Dr. Jacobsen looked at JoDee who shrugged her shoulders. She flipped through some notes. Christina watched her eyes ride back and forth across the pages.

"Well, now that we have a more complete picture, let's take a look at you."

Dr. Jacobsen grabbed her ophthalmoscope and looked into Christina's right eye. Christina focused on sitting still so as not to interrupt the doctor's examination. She sat and sat and sat. Dr. Jacobsen was looking in her eye a long time. Christina shifted her weight, as her seat fell asleep. With her slight movement, the paper on the examination table crinkled glaringly in the silent room. The doctor's exposed eye that had been shut through the exam, opened briefly, peeked at Christina, then closed again. Finally Dr. Jacobsen pulled back, only to swoop in again and look into Christina's left eye. Christina tried not to give into the temptation to blink. The doctor pulled away from Christina's left eye, and moved in on her right again. Then again in the left.

Christina blinked furiously when Dr. Jacobsen finally put the instrument in the pocket of her jacket. JoDee cleared her throat. Christina did too. Dr. Jacobsen said nothing. She pulled open a drawer in the cabinet next to the sink. Pulling out a popsicle stick, she commanded Christina to take off her shoes and socks.

Christina obeyed taking a quick whiff to see if her feet had developed an odor this morning. She lifted her foot onto the examination table. Dr. Jacobsen stood holding Christina's ankle. "I'm just going to run this stick down the bottom of your foot to check your nerve response."

JoDee stood up from her corner chair to watch. Dr. Jacobsen ran the popsicle stick from Christina's toes down her foot. Christina tried to suppress a laugh at the tickle. She also wanted to chuckle at the sight of her toes splaying backward toward her face, waving at her.

Dr. Jacobsen did the same to her other foot. These toes also waved at her.

Then Dr. Jacobsen put the stick in the garbage and sat down on the stool, facing Christina. JoDee sat down also.

"Well," Dr. Jacobsen started, her face more purposeful than Christina had ever seen it, "there's something going on in your brain."

Christina nodded. Dr. Jacobsen was looking right into her eyes, as if still looking for signs of something behind them.

"The nerve test I did on your feet shows that there is some damage to your neurological system. If I were to run a popsicle stick down my foot as I did to yours, my toes would curl." Dr. Jacobsen formed a fist with her hand to demonstrate the proper curl. "Your toes bent backward, which is a sign of neurological distress. And when I looked into your eyes I could see a swelling of the optic nerve, which is a clear indication that something is going on in your brain. So we need to have an MRI done to get a better picture of what we're dealing with here."

Christina looked at her mom with a smile. JoDee returned it.

"One thing it could be is a tumor on your pituitary gland."

Dr. Jacobsen's mention of a pituitary tumor seemed a step up from what Christina had come prepared to hear.

The doctor spent an unprecedented amount of time with Christina discussing a pituitary tumor: its likelihood of being cancerous, the not-open-brain surgery needed to remove it, the symptoms and risks.

"What else could we be looking at here?" JoDee asked.

"Well, there is a vast array of possibilities, that I..." Dr. Jacobsen tilted her head, choosing her words, "...I wouldn't recommend pursuing at this time. We don't know what it could be, so until we have a better idea, I just wouldn't go looking for all the paths this might take. That could be unnecessarily disturbing."

Christina and JoDee nodded their heads. The sentiment made sense. But Christina was curious why then they had spent all that time talking about a pituitary tumor.

Another good chunk of time was spent trying to schedule an MRI as soon as possible. The clinic had to coordinate with an imaging center and the soonest they could get Christina in was one week from that day. It was not satisfactory to JoDee, but at least they had ordered one.

Christina rode in the seat next to her mom away from the doctor's office. She watched the scenery blaze by her, her eyes fixed on one spot so that colorful blurs were all she could see of Portland.

*Give me Your eyes to see Lord.*

. . . . . . . . .

Christina sat on the deck of her parents' home in Port Angeles, looking out over the Strait of Juan de Fuca. It was Saturday evening, September 8th. Christina was home with her parents for the week between her doctor's appointment and her upcoming MRI. Her hometown was a place of great comfort for her. Her father always ran out with a beaming smile to greet her, carrying her bags in for her. Her mother took care of her and talked with her. She always went to her old church, where she was well-loved. It was a chance for her to let down and rest.

From her seat on the deck, Christina could see the sun descend upon the dark line of the ocean. Just before it reached the earth's edge, the lower half of the burning orb seemed to spill open, pouring its light out onto the surface of the Pacific Ocean. But it only lasted a moment, before the horizon swallowed the bottom half of the sun, and the upper half quickly diminished until a single wink was all that was left.

Christina sighed, thinking of the times in her youth when she and Jesse had stood on the trampoline and watched the sun slip into its nocturnal hibernation. They would jump as high as they could to catch one more brief stream of light, until finally, their jumping revealed nothing but the sun's leftovers.

That was back when she was young...and the sun's rays didn't shine upon the possibilities that she now faced.

She had spent the last several days in heavy thought. Every possibility had played out in vivid detail. Tumors, cancers, surgeries, life, death.

*What does it mean to be 25 and thinking about death?*

On deck chairs next to her sat Doug, JoDee, and Pastor Mike Jones, the pastor of Christina's childhood.

Pastor Mike was there to support and encourage the family... and to probe.

"So," he said gently in his deep voice, "you could be facing something really huge here Christina. Have you thought about that?"

Doug and JoDee looked at their daughter, awaiting her answer.

Christina nodded. "Yes, I have."

Pastor Mike waited for more.

Christina searched for the right words. "It could be something huge. But, to be honest, I'm ready...I'm ready to hear it...even if it's bad. This pain has been going on for so long now, it will honestly be a relief to put a name to it, do something about it... even if it kills me."

Pastor Mike nodded.

"It will just feel good to do something, know something...move forward... you know?"

Three heads nodded. Three faces looked contemplative.

Christina sighed, sad that her parents were having to deal with this mystery too. She wished she could ride down to Portland with her father that very moment, he with his box of tools, her with her ailment. They would walk into her life, he would whip out a wrench and a ruler, maybe a level, and after a good day's work, the problem would be fixed, the questions would be answered and the future would be secure. She knew her dad wanted to give that to her. And she wanted to give him the opportunity to do that for her.

But there was no handyman fix for this. They all were going to have to rely on God instead.

*I suppose that's the way it should be, isn't it Lord?* Christina mused. Please help my parents rely on You.

She thought about the wedding of family friends that she had missed that day because of a debilitating reaction to sitting in the hot tub the night before. She was supposed to play violin with her mom at that wedding. But she couldn't even get out of bed that morning. If she had gone, would people have looked at her any differently? What would they have said if they knew she might be dead in a month? Would they have said anything?

*I'm 25 and I might be dead in a month.*

Christina felt hot tears forming in the corners of her eyes. She took a big breath feeling three sets of eyes on her.

*I'm 25, God. And I'm alive today!*

• • • • • • • • •

Christina had her MRI on September 11th.

After forty minutes of jackhammers in her already pounding head, Christina stepped blinkingly into the light of the waiting room where Linsey and JoDee sat with one of JoDee's close friends from PA, Kim Mason, Pastor Mike's daughter. They all smiled at her approach.

"How did it go?" JoDee asked.

"Loud!" Christina said with a chuckle. "Really loud!" She tried to demonstrate the audio trauma by mouthing massive "Booms" and holding her hands over her ears. Her supporters chuckled at her pantomime. Just as Christina was climaxing her MRI demonstration with a whispered "Ahhhh!" eyes squeezed shut, body wrenched backward in agony, a quiet voice spoke behind Christina.

"Excuse me."

It was the technician; the chipper, friendly one who had helped calm Christina's nerves when she had first gotten there that morning. She seemed a little unsure of whether or not Christina was in pain in the lobby. Christina quickly dropped her hands and stood up straight, her face barely holding back her enjoyment at being caught in the act of goofiness.

"Hi," Christina said to break the tension.

In her hand, the technician held the worship CD Christina had listened to during the MRI. "Here's your CD."

The girl's eyes lingered on Christina's face, trying to match up the images she had been watching with the smiling face that she now saw.

"Thanks," Christina said with a big smile directed at the girl, as if to return the calming favor.

The girl left, and the group packed up to go.

• • • • • • • • •

Later that day, Christina's feet sat in a bowl of salted water. JoDee, Linsey and Kim were all sitting around her in cushy salon chairs, their feet also soaking in sweet-smelling bowls of water.

They had gone straight from the imaging center to get a yummy breakfast. And now they sat awaiting pedicures. They were told to expect the results of the MRI in a couple days. Two days of waiting. Might as well pass the time with a little pampering.

Ann, the woman who had gently placed Christina's feet in the bowl of water a few moments ago, gently toweled off the moisture on her feet. Workers did the same with the other women's feet as well, and they all prepared to be pedicured.

Christina's phone rang.

"Who could that be?" she said, feigning annoyance at the interruption. She looked at the screen, recognizing the number immediately. "It's my doctor's office."

Three concerned faces watched her answer the phone.

"Christina, this is Dr. Jacobsen."

Christina's eyes widened. "Hi."

"I have the results of your MRI here, and I wanted to call you right away. We think we see the reason for those headaches you've been having. There is a spot on your brain."

The room and all its activity seemed to fade away into the background. Christina was very aware of every sensation Ann's touch created in her feet, almost more aware of the feelings in her feet than of the meaning of the words in her ears.

"What we need you to do is go back to the imaging center and pick up your MRI slides. They're getting them ready for you. Take them across town to the office of Dr. Crowley – write this down...do you have a pen?"

"Uh," Christina pulled up her purse and dug around for a pen. Linsey whipped one in front of her face. "...yes, I've got a pen."

She wrote down the location of Dr. Crowley's office at Emanuel Hospital.

"We've already called them and told them you'll be coming by. They'll get you in for an appointment tomorrow."

"Okay," was all Christina could say.

"Do you understand?" Dr. Jacobsen was saying.

"I think so. So… I should do that today."

"Yes…today."

There was a pause on the line, and then: "He's an excellent surgeon…really… the best around here." Dr. Jacobsen seemed to be trying to reassure Christina of something. "Okay Christina?"

"O-Okay."

"Okay."

Christina felt the pause of uncertainty silencing both sides of the conversation.

"Thanks for getting back to me so soon," Christina finally said.

"Of course. We'll talk soon okay."

"Okay. Thanks Dr. Jacobsen."

Christina turned off her phone, keeping her eyes on it, unwilling to look into the eyes that bored anxiously into the silence she offered them. She put the phone in her purse, took a breath and looked at her mother.

"There's a spot on my brain."

Ann's nail file stopped mid-file. So did her three colleagues'.

JoDee's face slackened.

"We're supposed to pick up the film from the imaging center and take it to a neurosurgeon's office and set up an appointment for tomorrow."

They all continued to stare at her.

"Like, as soon as possible."

They leaped into action. JoDee paid Ann and her associates for what they had planned on doing. Kim cleaned up the area in which they had been lounging moments before. Linsey silently gathered her things and stood at the door, ready to lead the way. Christina thanked Ann, who was looking at Christina the way one would an injured bird.

The procession bolted out the door of the shop and loaded into JoDee's car, no one talking.

A flurry of anxious words finally touched down once they had the packet of film in the car with them.

"Should we?" Christina asked, her fingers gripping a sheet of film buried in the envelope. Her eyes passed over each member in the car, asking them to join her in levity.

"Yeah!" Linsey said.

Christina pulled one out gingerly. It was her brain...why shouldn't she look at pictures of it. She felt a moment of freedom in the unveiling of the evidence. For quite some time now, she had been gripped in a vise of unknowing. Now, she held in her own two hands the tangible proof of whatever it was that had invaded her body and her future.

She held the first film up to the light, careful to keep her fingers on the edge so as not to mar the picture. The sheet she had in hand was a quilt of side views of her brain. The images in the top left-hand corner showed a small outline of a head, complete with brain and jaw, eyeballs and teeth. As she perused through the rows of images, the brain grew larger and larger, from the progression of slices taken across her skull. Toward the lower right hand corner, the skull and brain got smaller again. Each shot of her brain simply looked like a blurry gray mass. She studied the cloud-like shapes. Was that it? Or that? No...that?

They passed around a few of the pictures, taking stabs at the shapes they saw. A lightness had filled the car again. The other ladies also seemed empowered by the understanding they could glean from the pictures, even though the images remained complete mysteries to their untrained eyes.

"Gosh, I never knew our brains were so cloudy-looking," Linsey said.

"Maybe yours isn't. Maybe just mine is. Maybe the whole cloud is a tumor," Christina offered.

"No, I don't think so Christina," JoDee insisted. "She said a spot. Just a spot."

"Besides, I think a brain full of clouds is better than a brain full of nothing," Kim offered.

"Although, we've always suspected I was a bit of an airhead."

They all laughed.

Within moments they held the envelope, inconspicuously closed again, before the reception desk of Dr. Crowley's office. There were two ladies behind the counter. One, a middle-aged woman with dyed-black hair and quarter-inch blonde roots at her scalp, was on the phone. The other, a young blonde woman, looked up at them.

JoDee handed the packet of film over the counter and said, "This is Christina Ahmann. Dr. Jacobsen said she called you guys and set up an appointment for Christina for tomorrow with Dr.

Crowley."

The blonde receptionist took the packet and said, in a very receptionist-type tone, "We'll see about that."

JoDee looked offended. "That's what Dr. Jacobsen told us over the phone."

The receptionist was looking at her computer screen. "Dr. Crowley is very busy." She began to click furiously with the mouse, moving it this way, click, that way, click, click, click. Each tap of her finger on the mouse seemed to give her face a harder edge. "I highly doubt we can get anybody in so quickly on such short notice."

At this point, the other lady behind the desk, who had by now hung up the phone, reached over and grabbed the packet of film from where her colleague had placed it on the counter. "Oh yes, we will! We'll get her in to see Dr. Crowley tomorrow."

Now it was the first receptionist's turn to look offended.

"I spoke with Dr. Jacobsen." the second receptionist said to her colleague. The blonde woman shrugged her shoulders and turned away.

Christina and her group all gathered closer to the second receptionist, who smiled kindly at Christina. "Hi sweetie." She then turned her attention to her own computer screen.

"Just let me see what we've got available." The painted white nail of her right pointer finger clicked on the mouse. "There's just not much free space tomorrow," she said, biting her lower lip.

"Dr. Jacobsen made it sound important," JoDee said.

"Oh..." the receptionist looked directly into JoDee's eyes, "...I understand. If it were my daughter, I would be doing everything I could to get her in right away." Her fingernail clacked more fiercely, chastising the screen for not showing any openings. Then both her hands ferociously tapped at the keyboard, pounding some motherly nurture into the unfeeling schedule of Dr. Crowley.

"Okay sweetie, I've made a spot for you tomorrow at 10 am with Dr. Crowley."

JoDee audibly sighed. "Thank you. Thank you so much." It was literally an answer to a prayer JoDee had prayed along the side of the road one day in Portland. "Lord, help us wade through the intimidating medical world." This felt like a miracle.

"Thank you," Christina said to the receptionist.

The woman looked at them, eyes soft. "He's the best," she said. "You're in good hands."

"Thank you," JoDee said, one mother to another.

"Thank you again." Christina said. Yes, I'm in good hands.

•  •  •  •  •  •  •  •  •

"Hi, I'm Drew." The young man shook Christina and JoDee's hands enthusiastically. "I'm Dr. Crowley's assistant." He was short and stocky, balding and smiling.

He wrapped the pressure cuff around Christina's arm, giving the cuff a gentle pat, as if to reassure her that this would be a simple procedure. Christina smiled kindly at him. As he squeezed the pump he said, "We'll get your vitals and do a couple of simple tests to check your neurological system."

Christina nodded.

After recording her blood pressure he pulled out his stethoscope and brought it to Christina's chest, which was exposed due to the low neckline of her T-shirt. He paused before touching her with it. He glanced from Christina's chest into her eyes, then said, "This might be kind of cold. Do you...want me to blow on it... to warm it up for you?"

Christina smiled, hurting for Drew for the embarrassment she caught in his eyes.

"Sure," she said lightly.

He opened his mouth and released a throaty breath onto the metal circle. His cheeks turned red as he blew. He didn't look into Christina's eyes again as he put the instrument against her skin and said, "I don't know if it did any good, but..."

Christina smiled and then focused on breathing properly for him. She glanced over at her mother who was grinning.

Drew led her through several tests on her eyes, her muscle strength, her gait and reflexes. He wrote something down after each test. Finally he turned to them and said, "So, have you seen your tumor?"

Christina looked up at him, surprised by his frankness.

"No."

"Do you want to see it?"

Christina looked at JoDee, who shrugged her shoulders.

"Yeah," Christina said, wondering if it was weird that she sounded so excited.

Drew pulled out the film Christina had already examined and placed it on the screen. He flipped the switch and an unnatural light blared off the wall with a buzz. Another matrix of grey clouds lit up. Drew studied it a moment, then pulled that sheet off, replacing it with another from the envelope. This one, they had not pulled from the packet in the car. There were several clear pictures of a brain, slices seen from the top down. But this brain had a thick, large smudge on it, like an enormous thumb had pressed thoughtlessly on the picture and left a heavy print behind. Drew's finger followed the edge of her brain. "This is the outline of your brain. We're looking down on it here, from the top." His finger moved to the white bulge in the right quadrant. "And this..." his finger outlined the shape, "is your tumor."

Christina stared at the cloudy orb, fascinated. There it was: the reason for all the weird things she had been feeling this past year, the cause of this uncomfortable drama in her life, the shape of the unknown.

It was large: the size of a racquetball... not a 'spot' as Dr. Jacobsen had said on the phone...this was a mass! Her brain looked crowded and uncomfortable in its presence. How had she been functioning all this time with that massive brute pressing into her thoughts? It took Christina's breath away to see it so clearly. It seemed a living, breathing enemy to her way of life, glaring at her from the buzzing screen...a serpent, curled up in her head.

"It's big," JoDee said, voicing Christina's thoughts.

"It's huge," Drew confirmed. "This is a very large tumor. We're amazed that you haven't had more symptoms than what you've listed. I mean, it's really phenomenal. The fact that you haven't had a seizure...it's..." Drew shook his head.

"...A miracle," JoDee finished for him.

"Yeah," Drew said, nodding his head.

Christina smiled at him. Show yourself to Drew Lord.

"I'll get Dr. Crowley for you," he said, his eyes passing over the images one more time before he left the room.

Christina and JoDee were alone in the room with the buzzing screen. They sat directly across from each other, alternately staring into each other's eyes and up at the screen.

"There. I've seen it," Christina said. "A tumor. I still feel great!" she said in all honesty. JoDee's eyes widened and then she nodded.

"How do you feel?"

JoDee nodded slowly. "I feel okay. I really feel okay."

Christina nodded. "I mean, it's weird, seeing it there. But, at the same time, it's like I'm finally getting to look at something that I think has been real to me for quite some time...you know? And I'm okay with it. God has brought me to this point...prepared me for this. I'm just following His lead."

JoDee nodded.

Dr. Crowley walked into the room, a white-clad, clean-cut image of doctor smarts. He took Christina's hand in a soft gentle handshake, his handsome blue eyes studying her.

He turned to the images with the casualness of a mechanic approaching a broken-down Ford. "I see you've seen the tumor."

Christina nodded.

"It's a large tumor," he stated gently, turning back to her, looking at her as a person.

"So we've been told," Christina said.

"We can see that," JoDee said at the same time.

Christina and JoDee smiled at him.

Dr. Crowley's eyes flickered for a moment.

"It's really amazing that you haven't experienced any other symptoms than headaches and double vision."

Christina nodded again. She looked at JoDee, whose eyes were locked on hers.

"Which is a good sign. Based on your symptoms, my guess is that this is a slow-growing benign tumor. Usually, the cancerous tumors grow quickly and result in more drastic symptoms, such as seizures. I would say this one," he touched the cloud on the screen, "has been in there for a long time, and your brain has been slowly adjusting to its presence, forming new pathways around it. It seems pretty likely that this is a meningioma...a tumor that grows in the outer layer of the brain tissue. And those kinds of tumors are well contained with clearly defined borders... quite easy to remove."

Christina grasped onto the hope in Dr. Crowley's voice.

"What other kinds of tumors are there?" JoDee asked.

Dr. Crowley shook his head, switching roles from doctor to psychiatrist. "Oh, there are many different types of brain tumors...about 100. My suggestion to you is to avoid researching the different types, online or anywhere else...it will just open up a whole world of discouraging possibilities. Until we know for sure what we're dealing with, there's really no point in preparing for something that it's not."

41

Christina and JoDee nodded again.

"Of course, there's no way for us to know for sure what kind of tumor it is without getting it out and having a biopsy done. Different tumors have different textures, which we cannot determine from MRI imaging. We need to see it firsthand. And we need to get it out as soon as possible. With its size, you are at high risk for seizures. The sooner we can relieve your brain of the enormous pressure it's under, the better. Fortunately, this tumor is in a place where we can operate with minimal risk to your brain's function. But, as with any open brain surgery, there are several risks...we'll want to go over all of those carefully."

Dr. Crowley prescribed a drug to reduce her chances of a seizure and fight the fatigue she constantly felt. They quickly dubbed it the Tumor Pill. He outlined the procedure she would be having, the risks, the results, the possibilities after it. He answered her and JoDee's questions as best he could. As she listened, Christina mostly did a lot of nodding and 'mmm-hmmm'ing.

Several times, Dr. Crowley would repeat something he had just said, phrasing it a little differently, obviously trying to make sure Christina understood what he was saying. And she would just nod again. She could see him forming a thought about her: Clearly this girl doesn't understand the gravity of this situation. Poor thing.

But Christina understood fully.

Okay Lord. This is the next step, huh? We've been through so much this past year... This is what You were preparing me for. Okay Lord. I will go with You

She held the staff of the Lord in her hand.

# An Encounter in the Wilderness

*So my question for you is...What do you fear in life? Our fears correlate very directly to our trust in God. Do we believe that He is enough? Do we believe He will truly supply every need like He says? My prayer for you (you can pray this for me as well)...is that you can live a life FREE of the bondage of fear. I pray that as you face your list of fears and insecurities, you can take every last one of those issues to the feet of Jesus asking for strength to trust Him. Because let me tell you friends, we serve a trustworthy God.*

*Love,*

*Christina*

Moses was a peaceful shepherd in Midian, obscure and unimportant in the world. Over the last forty years, he had grown to like his quiet life in the wilderness. It was secure, predictable, safe. It might not have been what he had imagined for himself back when he was a young lad growing up in the palaces of Egypt. But, if asked, he would have said, "I'm happy."

That was about to change.

One day, Moses was going about his usual duties in the quiet expanse of the dusty, dry wilderness: mentally tallying his father-in-law's sheep, keeping an eye out for danger among the thorny desert bushes, occasionally taking off his sandals to clear out a jagged pebble. He dreamt happily of the homecoming his family would give him when he returned to their goatskin tent next week. His sons would run out and shout "Papa." Moses would scoop them up in bear hugs. Then he would hold his lovely wife in a long warm embrace. A smile lit upon his face at the thought.

Then Moses saw a flicker of light out the corner of his eye. He walked toward the source, finding himself drawn by something greater than curiosity. His eyes saw a bush that seemed to be on fire. As random as that sight would be in the desert, what was even stranger was the nature of the fire. It was active, with white hot flames licking up the sides of the bush and disappearing into shimmering vapors in the air overhead. But the fire seemed to consume nothing, for the bush didn't change shape or texture in its flaming envelope. Green, bristly branches still swayed within the fiery orb. The fire seemed to be an extension of the bush: root, stem, branch, leaf, flame of fire.

Moses cautiously approached the scene.

Suddenly, a Voice emanated from the bush, Voice unmistakable, a Voice from beyond the edges of the world.

"Moses! Moses!"

Unsure of what else to do, Moses answered with a shaky, "I'm here."

"Don't come any closer," the Voice from the bush boomed.

Moses stopped immediately, his eyes burning from the brightness of the white flames.

"Take off your sandals, for the place where you are standing is holy ground."

Moses sat down on a nearby stone and began to remove his sandals. He kept throwing squinty glances at the bush, waiting for it to identify itself. But, Moses knew in his heart whose Voice spoke from the bush.

"I am the God of your father, the God of Abraham, the God of Isaac and the God of Jacob." The bush quivered with each word that qualified its Creator.

Moses immediately grabbed a fold of his scratchy robe and held it before his face; for ancient tradition held that one does not see the face of the Lord and live to speak of it. He peeked fearfully around his tattered robe, wondering what would prompt the God of his fathers to speak to him.

"Moses, I have seen the misery of my people." With these words, the bush dripped flaming tears down onto the dusty earth where they disappeared in a puff of smoke. "I've heard their cries from Egypt. And I'm sending you to go before Pharaoh and demand that he release my people."

Moses released his cloak, holding his shaky hands before him in a pose of supplication. His face reflected his horror.

Return to Egypt! Moses pictured himself, 80-years-old and increasingly introverted, leaving his quiet life in Midian and traipsing back to Egypt, the land that had exiled him. He imagined going before the people of Jacob, the ones who had mocked him forty years ago. He imagined going before Pharaoh and demanding that the most powerful ruler in the world release his work force. Did God know what He was asking? Moses would have laughed at the utter inanity of the thought if he wasn't in the presence of the Most Holy One.

"Me Lord?" He looked at the air above the bush. "Are you joking? Who am I? Why would Pharaoh do what I ask of him?"

"I will be with you Moses." Each word that passed from the bush seemed to float toward him on a calm flame. "I give you this guarantee that I am your Source: when you come out of Egypt with my people, you will come here and worship Me on this mountain."

Now the Lord was speaking about this ridiculous idea as if it were a certainty. Moses certainly would deliver the Lord's people, and he certainly would lead them back to this mountain to worship God. Now Moses' fear turned into panic.

"Well, who exactly are You?" he asked, too distraught to wonder if he should argue with God. "If the Hebrews ask who sent me, what should I say?"

Patiently, graciously, the Lord answered. "I AM WHO I AM. You tell the Hebrew leaders that I AM has sent you."

"But..." Moses wasn't even listening at this point. He was just spouting off arguments as quickly as they came to him. "What if they don't believe me?" Moses' last encounter with the Hebrews had not gone well. Forty years prior Moses had stepped up, albeit immorally, on behalf of one of his marginalized brethren. His people had reacted by ridiculing and challenging him...rejecting him. Moses had no clout with the Hebrews. Why should they ever follow him?

45

"What if they don't believe me?" Moses asked again.

"What's that in your hand?" A lone flame flashed outward, pointing at the staff in Moses' hand.

"A staff."

"Throw it to the ground."

Moses glanced skeptically at the air above the bush, then threw his rod to the ground. Immediately, the staff began to slither figure eights in the dirt at his feet.

Moses screamed and ran behind a large boulder. It was a cobra, the revered snake of Egypt. He hadn't seen one in over forty years. He peeked his head around the rock. The snake had coiled at the base of the bush. Moses took a tentative step out from behind the rock, never taking his eyes off the snake.

"Reach out your hand and take it by the tail."

Moses shook his head, his mouth open in amazement. Any man knew that one does not ever grab a snake by the tail. If you have to grab one, you subdue it with a stick and then hold it behind the triangular head so it cannot strike at you.

The bush waved gently, calling Moses forward.

Moses took a step. The cobra watched him, its wedge head vacillating in the air. Moses walked slowly toward it, watching its eyes, its flaring nostrils. The snake's stringy forked tongue licked at the air.

Moses brought his trembling hand to the snake's body, stretching his fingers to grasp the cobra's tail. Feeling the dry, waxy skin of the snake, Moses quickly closed his violently shaking hand. At contact, the snake lengthened and stiffened, becoming the staff once again.

Still shaking all over, Moses stood erect. His hand loosely held the inert staff, as though worried it might awaken again.

The Voice from the bush led Moses through another miracle involving a leprous hand. Moses mindlessly followed the instructions, watching in horror as his hand sickened before his very eyes.

It was all a blur to him, a terrifying cacophony of sounds and images. What he was seeing terrified him. But not as much as the calling these signs pointed him toward.

"Lord, I'm not very eloquent," he tried again.

The bush seemed to sigh. "Who gave you your mouth? Is it not I who makes a man eloquent? Go. I will help you speak and teach you what to say."

Moses was running out of arguments. But he knew in the depths of his heart that he did not want to do what the Lord was asking. It was too hard. It was too scary. He could be embarrassed. He could be hurt. He could die! And what about his family? They had a good life here. They were comfortable. Why would the Lord require them to leave their comforts? Why make them abandon all they'd known and enter a very dark uncertainty? It was too much. Moses couldn't take it.

"Oh Lord, please send someone else. I don't want to do it!"

The bush exploded in a blinding splash of hot, burning fire. The ground rumbled and rolled. A crack formed in the granite below the ground's sandy blanket. The branches of the bush, so green at first, were now illuminated in a brilliance that burned Moses' eyes even when he wasn't looking right at them. Moses himself was thrown down to the ground, and as the world shook around him, a heavy hand seemed to be pressing down on his body, holding him firm, a helpless observer to the destruction around him.

The storm of God's anger raged for several moments, deafening and wonderful.

Finally, the earth lay down, the sand settled over the quiet stones, the wind sighed softly and the bush returned to its previous state of perpetual burn.

Moses lay face down on the ground sobbing loudly. He felt naked...stripped of everything in this world he had ever found comforting.

Eventually the Voice spoke again.

With his face pressed into the sand, tears spilling out from clamped eyelids, Moses listened to the Lord telling him to go to Egypt, promising him that his brother Aaron would accompany him, even speak for him.

Then a silence hung in the air.

Moses opened his eyes to see the bush watching him, gentle flames waving.

"Now take the staff Moses. Do my wonders."

The bush flamed out. The green branches went still, as if in shock.

Moses lay in the dirt for a long time, weeping.

He played through the many scenarios he could face if he did indeed return to Egypt. He felt the pain, the humiliation, the fear;

and he wept over it all.

Finally, spent and weak, Moses leaned against the staff, pulling himself up by its sturdy strength.

Moses led his sheep back to his family in Midian. As he walked, he entertained notions of how to get out of his predicament: running away, staying put and simply refusing to go, begging one more time. Moses played out each scenario.

Without the drama of the bush, the Lord continued to converse with Moses, in the still, quiet voice of the Spirit. The Lord knew what He was doing. He had prepared Moses. Moses' life was an 80-year education, equipping him for the very call he was loathe to answer. The first forty years of his life he had spent in the courts of Egypt, studying their laws, their beliefs, their politics, their way of life. He was no stranger to the system that placed the Pharaoh amongst the pantheon of the gods. The other 40 years of Moses' life were spent as a resident of the wilderness, leaving him well prepared to lead the Hebrews through it.

But God wouldn't make the decision for Moses. He would argue with him, comfort him, reassure him, but ultimately, Moses had to make the choice to follow God. A willing servant is more precious and useful to God than a slave.

Moses went back to his tent. He told his wife what the Lord had asked him to do. Zipporah was skeptical. They discussed it for several days.

Moses approached his father-in-law, expecting a resistance from Jethro that matched his own.

"Jethro...let me take your daughter and grandchildren and go back to Egypt, back to my people. I want to see if any of them are still alive."

Jethro grabbed Moses' shoulders and said lovingly, "Go, and I wish you well. Shalom."

Moses walked away from that encounter surprised by Jethro's answer.

He holed up in his tent for days, slowly packing their belongings... feeling compelled to do so, even though he had yet to give God a definitive answer.

Through all the toiling, Moses heard the Lord asking him one question over and over:

*Moses, am I enough?*

*If you are embarrassed...if the Hebrew people laugh in your face and turn their backs on you, am I enough for you? Can you still follow me with joy into the path I have planned out for you?*

*If Pharaoh draws you in and then has you beaten and imprisoned, am I enough for you?*

*If you die... if your family leaves you... if you lose the life you've come to love, am I enough for you? Can you surrender all the things of this world and serve Me because I am the only thing that is truly everlasting?*

It took a while for Moses to get there, but eventually he packed everything up, said his goodbyes, "And Moses took the staff of God in his hand."

That was his answer.

*Yes Lord! You are enough! I will follow You with joy no matter where I find myself.*

Moses walked to Egypt, ready for what awaited him there.

# The Summer Prior

Christina woke up in pain. Lots of pain.

*Not again! Lord! Please!*

She rolled over, hoping the pull of sleep would be stronger than the rage of pain in her head. She stretched her legs out, her feet searching for the comfort of a cool spot in the sheets. She placed pillow number two between her legs, and leaned her body against pillow number three. No good...she rolled over again, bringing the pillows over with her.

Her entire head pulsed violently. Each beat of her heart pounded against her skull, leaving an ache in its place until a new beat rocked her again, and again and again. There was no escaping it. The pounding was too loud...too strong...too painful. She could no longer hear the anxious call of sleep.

She pried her eyes open.

5:45 in the morning. Christina, never an early riser, had been getting used to the hours of O-dark-thirty: the stillness, the chill, the isolation.

She sat up in bed, the pounding growing in her head. She was so tired, but she knew it was pointless to try to grasp at sleep again... more than pointless... it was painful. After several months of intermittently getting these morning headaches, she was aware that lying around just seemed to make it worse; getting up was the only thing that helped.

She stepped carefully onto the floor, her eyelids gritty against her bleary eyes. She shuffled out of her room. Even in her sleepy state, she was sensitive to the need to be quiet so as not to awaken Linsey. The light of day was beginning to turn the sky an aqua blue. Christina's legs obeyed her commands to walk forward, but small steps were all she could muster. She moved from the carpeted living room to the linoleum of the kitchen. Crumbs pricked the bottoms of her feet. Another step landed her foot in something sticky...jam undoubtedly. A sudden realization sent her blood coursing through her body at more volume: she hadn't washed the floor this week. Linsey had asked her twice, and she still hadn't done it. Her remorse caused her heart to beat faster, and her head to hurt more.

Slowly, painfully, she walked into the kitchen, still cluttered and dirty from the movie night that had ended just six hours before.

The espresso maker was hidden behind a pile of dirty bowls and cloudy glasses. Christina wasn't sure her fingers would be as obedient as her legs if she were to try to make a latte.

She leaned one arm against the kitchen counter. Her other arm followed and both hands gripped the countertop.

Pound, pound, pound.

Her fingers clutched more tightly, trying to match the grip of the vise that had a hold of her head.

If it weren't for the attention the pain demanded, Christina felt like she could almost fall asleep standing right there in the semi-dark, like a cow.

"Christina?"

She forced her eyes to open, blinking against the bright kitchen lights that Linsey had just turned on. Her roommate stood looking at her with concern, and a touch of humor.

"What are you doing?"

"Waiting for my headache to go away," Christina said through a grimace, not releasing her desperate grip on the countertop.

"Aaah... another one?" Linsey said bustling into the kitchen, sweeping the dirty dishes into the sink and awakening the espresso maker. "Ever since I've known you, you've gotten headaches, headaches, and more headaches."

Not like these, Christina thought.

"How do you stand it?" Linsey continued.

*I can't.*

Linsey started rinsing the dishes in the sink and preparing a breakfast of eggs. "Brett's massage last night didn't help ease the tension in your neck, huh?"

"Guess not," Christina said, watching Linsey tidy up the mess. The pounding was lessening. She grabbed a couple dishes and started drying them, to contribute.

"This is ridiculous Christina. What is wrong with your tense little neck? You must be working too hard."

Christina sighed at the suggestion. As if.

"Why won't you try a new pillow, like I've suggested?" Linsey asked.

Christina thought about the money she did not have to buy a new pillow. "I don't think it will help."

"Well, what is helping you, huh? Nothing. You've had a lot of these lately, and all the massages your man is giving you just don't

51

seem to be making a difference. So, you might as well try a new pillow. It certainly can't make it any worse. Look, after my meeting this morning, I'm taking you to Bed, Bath and Beyond to get a new pillow. No arguing!"

Christina shrugged her tight shoulders, no energy for argument.

Linsey waved a latte under Christina's nose, causing a wave of warmth and scent to scale Christina's wall of pain. She gratefully grabbed the cup. "Thanks," she said, her voice finally sounding like her. She took a gentle sip of the hot liquid, swallowing hard. A sliver of sunshine was shining over the top of the fence in the backyard. Christina watched the light invade the house, feeling its light pierce the devastation of her morning routine.

What is wrong with me Lord? Her heart cried out for answers that simply weren't coming.

*Will you follow Me Christina?*
*Yes…but…Lord…what's wrong with me?*

· · · · · · · · ·

"Don't!!"

Christina awoke from a deep snooze, reorienting herself on the couch.

"You don't!" Christina said weakly, returning the greeting. She rubbed her eyes, feeling groggy. Her watch informed her that she had slept for two hours. And now Linsey was back from selling buttons, supporting her life and the life of her friend. Christina felt bad. I sleep the morning away, and Linsey goes off to take on the world. Lord?!

"Your headache gone?" Linsey asked from her room, where she was putting away her business materials and logging information on her computer.

"Pretty much, yeah," Christina said, rising to check the tension in her neck and shoulders. She did a couple neck rolls…not too bad. Her head felt more clear, more capable. She walked to the bathroom to match her look to her improved mood. Watching herself in the mirror she pulled her tousled hair back in a ponytail. She patted her cheeks, where the lines of the couch reminded her of her wasted morning. She sighed at the endless pileup of wasted mornings that her life seemed to be becoming.

Linsey bounced into the bathroom, her face flush with a morning well spent.

"Ready to go to Bed, Bath and Beyond...get the Teeners a new pillow? A 'take-all-my-neck-tension-away' pillow?" Linsey was squeaking with The Voice. "Nooo more tension. Nooo more tension." She was pinching at Christina's neck as she spoke. "Awaieee! Awaiieeee! Tension go awaieee!"

Christina smiled at her friend's hammin', wondering how much a 'take-all-my-neck-tension-away' pillow went for these days.

Linsey left the bathroom with a sing-songy, "Bye-bye tension."

Christina turned back to the mirror, her smile dropping off her face.

"Let's get lattes on the way," Linsey called from the kitchen.

Christina grimaced. "Linsey, I can't get a latte." She walked dejectedly to the kitchen.

"My treat," Linsey said quickly. "I got another account today. It's my celebration latte."

"Wow! Good for you!" Christina said, truly joyful for her roommate's success. "That's so great. You're just knockin' 'em down this year aren't you?"

"It's the year of the buttons for Linsey Tuttle."

"Yeah," Christina echoed in The Voice, "buttons and moooooollaaaaah."

"Moollah for lattes."

Christina shook her head. "Are you sure?"

"Would I offer if I wasn't?"

"No, you would not." Christina shrugged again. "Far be it from me to rob you of your celebration latte."

"Or make me drink it alone. What's a celebration latte if it isn't shared?"

"Well, what are we waiting for then?"

"I'll drive," Linsey called over her shoulder, her ponytail bouncing with anticipation, much like Linsey did.

On the car ride, Christina regretfully broached a topic she hated.

"Linsey, I know the month of April came and went and I never paid you the rest of the rent."

"Teena, it's okay. You weeded the flower bed last week. We'll call it even."

Christina sighed. "LIN-sey...."

"TEE-na! If I needed the money, I would make you square up. But it's okay. You need a little financial grace right now and I am

53

able and more than willing to give it to you."

"But, I don't have all of May's rent yet either."

"I know. It's okay. We'll see how your month goes. Maybe God's got some big surprises for you Tuh. You never know. Let's just wait and see what He does before we set anything down."

Christina sighed again. "I don't want you to feel like I'm taking advantage of your generosity."

"I don't," Linsey said emphatically. She touched Christina's knee, taking her eyes off the road long enough to gently reassure Christina with a look. "I don't."

Christina nodded. "You don't."

"No, you don't!" Linsey Voiced back.

"No! You don't!"

Then it went quiet again.

Linsey sighed. "Teena, it takes a long time to get a business up and going, you know. You can't expect it to be a success right away."

"It's been a year, and I'm no better than I was when I started. In fact, I think I'm worse off than when I started."

"It takes time Teena. You have to be patient. God will provide."

Christina was silent, thinking back on the year. Did God provide this past year? I'm in debt, accruing more every month. And the clients simply aren't coming. Is that God's provision? Christina could hear the bitterness in her thought. They seemed to sear through her brain leaving a path of pain in her head. Bitterness was so unlike her. But it wasn't God with whom she was upset; it was herself. Sometimes, though, her disappointment landed on the wrong subject.

"Tell you what," Linsey interrupted Christina's thoughts. "When we get back home, I'll help you work on your business cards. And we'll print up a new batch of coupons for you to take with you when you go to the fitness center to market. 'Kay?"

"'Kay," Christina said, a little grumpily. Those business cards she had been intending to make for months now. Linsey had practically offered to do them for her several times. Maybe I should just let her make them for me after all. Obviously, I'm not getting to them. She'll make them so much better than I ever could anyway.

Christina watched the world flash past her in the window, a spectator in Linsey's car…a spectator in life.

*Will you follow Me Christina?*
*What does that mean Lord?*

· · · · · · · ·

"Here try this one." Linsey held a contour pillow up for Christina's perusal. Christina grabbed the pillow, scanning the price tag before placing her head against its concave surface.

"Yeah, it's nice."

"You can't get a feel for it standing up," Linsey exclaimed.

*Why not, I spend half my nights standing up.*

"You're right." Christina promptly dropped the pillow on the floor. "Could you grab me one of those down comforters off the bed over there?"

Linsey laughed. "And a nightgown?"

"And a teddy bear?"

Christina lowered to the floor and lay back onto the pillow. A lady browsing through the bed sheets watched Christina lay down and smiled.

The pillow was nice. It did seem to support her neck in a way that her own did not...her tension-filled neck.

Linsey had her cell phone up in the air, aiming it at her lying on the floor at Bed Bath and Beyond. "Smile Tuh!"

Christina smiled big for the click. Then she closed her eyes for another. Then she rolled onto her side, folding her legs up to her chest. Click. Click.

"Oooh, Teena. This one says it was designed by NASA!" Linsey was holding another pillow, shaped just like the one Christina now rested her head against. But this particular pillow looked expensive. It was Godiva chocolate to the Hershey's pillow Christina currently rested against. She lifted her head and placed it on the Godiva pillow. It seemed to melt and mold to the contours of her head and neck. It felt great.

She sighed contentedly. "This feels nice."

"Yeah, well, NASA. I would hope they know what they're doing."

Christina sat up and checked the price tag of the Godiva pillow: $100!

"A hundred bucks! For a pillow!"

Linsey shrugged. "Too much?"

"For a pillow!?"

"What's the other one cost?"

"Thirty bucks."

"Yeah, but does the NASA pillow feel better?"

"It doesn't matter Linsey, I can't spend $100 on a pillow. I'll just get this one." She grabbed the Hershey pillow, replacing the Godiva one.

"All right," Linsey said. "One 'take-all-Teeners-neck-tension-away' pillow comin' right up."

They went to the front counter where Christina charged the pillow to her credit card. She grimaced as she slid the card, knowing her debts were increasing with this purchase. Lord, please help me get some work. I need clients Lord. I need clients.

A nasty voice whispered in her heart, "Well, if you'd stop sleeping away your mornings and buying pillows you don't need, you might not be in this situation."

Christina sighed, feeling the heaviness of her inadequacies.

Linsey, weighted down by bags of goodies she had bought at Mariposa before the pillow purchase, led the way back to the parking lot.

"So, how are things with Brett?" Linsey asked.

"Oh...you know."

"No, I don't know."

Christina sighed. "Oh, not so good."

"Tuh! What's going on?"

"I don't know. I really don't know. I'm meeting with the pastor's wife next week to talk about it."

"Do you think you guys aren't going to make it?" Linsey asked sadly.

"I don't know...I don't know."

"Oh," Linsey moaned, "it would be so, so sad if you guys broke up. What about our double dates? Who are Robbie and I supposed to hang out with?"

"Oh no!" Christina feigned with The Voice. "You'll be soo lonely!"

Linsey tapped Christina's arm. "I just want us all to be together."

"You'll be okay. Besides, we haven't broken up yet." ...yet.

• • • • • • • •

It was a beautiful 4th of July. A day of celebration, a day of family and friends, hot dogs, fireworks, drinks and laughter.

Portland was alive with happy fellowship.

Christina, however, was alone except for the dog Lucy and her catawampus ears.

It was late afternoon. She had farewelled Linsey and Robbie about an hour ago as they went off to a barbecue with Robbie's co-workers.

"I'm sure you could come," Linsey had practically begged, not wanting to leave Christina alone.

"No, no." Christina had assured her. "I wouldn't know anybody, and nobody would know me. I would feel so lame. 'Who's the girl wandering around like a lost puppy?'" Christina imagined aloud. "'Someone call the Pound.'"

"No one would think that," Linsey said.

"I would!"

"What will you do then?"

"I might call someone, see if there're any raging parties for me to crash...Go entertain everyone with my charm and wit." Christina spread her hands wide at her sides in a showy stance.

"Are you sure?" Linsey asked, sorrow on her face.

"I'm fine! Go, have fun. Go on now kids." She shooed Robbie and Linsey out the door.

"Don't!" Linsey had called as she walked out to the car.

"You don't!" Christina had called back.

Now, alone in the house, the Silence was a presence she could feel in each and every room. Lucy was napping on the couch, her gentle breaths inaudible. Christina grabbed her IPod and walked out into the noisy neighborhood. She walked and walked. Yards were filled with children and smoky, fragrant barbecues. Lawn chairs held lounging people, laughter bouncing between them and out to Christina, almost seeming to mock her loneliness.

This was not how she had planned to spend this day. She and Brett were supposed to be together in Bend, Oregon at an Allison Krauss concert. But, typically, you don't go to concerts with a boyfriend once he becomes an ex-boyfriend.

It had only been a few days since they had broken up, but Christina was still adjusting to the notion of life without Brett. They had spent 8 months getting to know each other, connecting pieces of their lives and futures, filling each others' hours and space with companionship and hope.

Now those spaces were as empty as the space at Christina's side where the Silence now was.

She waved confidently to the neighbors, trying not to look as lame as she felt, walking around the neighborhood alone on the 4th of July. Good thinking Christina! Walk through the neighborhood alone, past all their barbecues. Nice!

She took the shorter route back to the house. Lucy still slept on the couch, her eyes only peeking open to acknowledge her return. Christina called a couple friends, but no gatherings sparked her fancy. Too much explaining to do.

*I'm alone on the Fourth of July. I'm going to make the most of it doggonit. I can spend a day alone...what's the big deal?*

"Dinner," she said aloud. "What should I have for dinner?"

She opened the fridge, seeing some aging leftovers and a few vegetables.

"Enchiladas," she decided. With Linsey gone, she could make them as hot and spicy as she wanted.

But the house didn't hold all she needed to make enchiladas so she hopped in her car and drove down the road to Safeway. She walked past several Fourth of July displays as she searched for jalapenos, enchilada sauce and chicken. Balloons were all over. People were grabbing chips, hot dogs... collecting last minute contributions for the parties to which they were headed.

Christina bought her items and walked out to her car. The fireworks stand at the back of the parking lot was busy with shoppers. Christina smiled to herself and walked towards it.

*Why shouldn't I have a couple fireworks for myself on the Fourth of July, huh? It's the birth of our country for Pete's sake.*

She bought a package of sparklers, shrugging her shoulders at the outrageous price.

Back at the house, she built her enchiladas, throwing in extra jalapenos. While they cooked, she walked out into the backyard. The sun was losing its influence behind the oak trees. She built a fire, letting its warmth make up for the sun's missing rays. Longing for more light to fill the spaces around her she lit up the tiki torches. But it still wasn't enough. She scoured the house, finding every candle she could, lighting them and arranging them outside in a circle around the deck chairs.

There, she thought, wondering what exactly it was she sought.

She scooped a pile of spicy enchiladas onto a plate, took it outside, and sat down in the ring of light, around the warm fire.

But the candles couldn't chase away her loneliness. Her eyes felt hot. She blinked hard, not wanting to cry by herself on the Fourth of July.

*Get a grip Christina. You're okay. You're okay. I've still got the Lord.*

She pulled her shoulders back and down, away from the pinching they liked to do up to her ears. The tension was building, and her head was beginning to pound.

*Relax.*

"Sparklers," she said, jumping to her feet.

She retrieved the package from the house and lit one. It jumped to flame, twitching and flashing bright, frenetic lights. Christina waved it around. She spelled out her name, watching each letter disappear as quickly as she wrote it. She laughed at the ridiculousness of her situation. She finished her name and the sparkler still vibrated in her hand. Unsure what else to do with it, she stared into its aggressive flames until it piddled away to nothing.

The darkness had settled in for good now, and Christina was beginning to feel cold. She grabbed a blanket from inside, wrapped herself into it, and sat down on the deck chair. The neighbors were beginning to light their fireworks, and every once in a while a red or blue rocket would pierce the darkness over the backyard fence. Christina would follow its path until it too yielded to the pitch black.

*What Lord? What do you have for me? Am I to live my life alone? Am I too picky? Is there not a man out there who can share a life with me?*

*Will you follow Me Christina?*

*Yes...but...*

The heat was returning to her eyes. She blinked again.

On her own, facing a mountain of bills, a floundering career, men who weren't right for her, and the dangers of comparison, Christina found herself balking at the reality of faith in the world. Is this all there is Lord? Is this really my life?

*Will you follow Me Christina?*

*I don't know God...*

Her head started pounding at the approach of her tears.

She blinked harder and tried to relax her shoulders. I just don't know God...

Just then, the back door opened.

"There you are!"

It was the most glorious sound Christina had ever heard.

"You didn't answer my 'don'ts' and the whole house was pitch black...but your car was here...so I figured you were here, I just couldn't find you. Look at you out here with a nice little set-up... candles, fire, dinner..." Linsey held up the plate of unfinished enchiladas. "Having a nice time?"

Christina wiped her face to make sure no renegade tears had escaped her notice. "Hey, how was your barbecue?"

Linsey pulled up the other deck chair. "Ugh, terrible! Robbie was having one of his doubting days again."

"Uh oh!" It was so nice to have something to think about other than her own loneliness.

"But wait," Linsey said, "what have you been doing? Did you go anywhere?"

Back to her loneliness. "No, I just stayed home." The heat was returning.

"Teena! I thought you were going to go somewhere! You've been alone all this time?!"

There was no stopping the tears now. Afraid her voice would crack, Christina didn't say anything.

But Linsey knew.

"Teena!" And Linsey's voice cracked. "I'm sorry! I didn't want you to be alone today. Are you okay? I'm so sorry."

Linsey reached over and hugged Christina hard. Christina couldn't stop the crying now...not with Linsey holding the emotions all out before them like a burnt marshmallow.

They cried together for a minute.

"I'm so sorry you were alone," Linsey said again. "I should have stayed with you. It would have been more fun...believe me!" She wiped her eyes, switching over to her 'annoyed with Robbie' voice.

"Tell me what happened," Christina said as she wiped her eyes. And even through the tears, Christina was happier than she had been all day.

• • • • • • • • •

A sweaty man opened the doors of the gym and strode towards Christina. He walked on the balls of his feet, as if his calf workout was just beginning. He was huge. His sleeveless shirt stuck to his

60

body, evidence of the sweating he had done. Massive pectoral muscles bounced with each step. Christina tried not to let her face visibly react to the sight of the swollen biceps, the meaty shoulders, the neck the size of her thighs with cords as tight as coconut husks. He lifted up his shirt to give his sweaty brow a cleansing swipe, or just to show off his quilted abs. As he released his shirt, Christina saw he was looking at her.

She stood up quickly, trying to drape her professionalism over the awkwardness of the moment.

"Excuse me," she said, realizing it was a pointless statement since he was already fully aware of her, "would you like a free 10 minute massage?"

He smiled widely, seeing the massage chair next to Christina.

"Heck yeah!" he practically snorted.

"Great!" Christina said, forcing enthusiasm into the word. "Why don't you have a seat. My name is Christina. I have a clinic over on SW Parkway."

He leaned his massive chest into the massage chair, laying his sweaty face onto the head rest. "So what are you doing here?" he mumbled into the cushy hole. "Trying to get new clients?"

"Basically," Christina said. "Just trying to get my name out there, ya know."

"Cool."

Christina rubbed the massage lotion in between her hands to warm it. She eyed his enormous neck like it was an enemy. She ran her fingers down his trapezius. Just as she thought: thick, unwieldy and tight. She pressed harder.

And it all hurt.

The exertion sent her blood pounding, directly into her head. Her neck seized, pulling her shoulders forward and upward. Her arms and fingers wanted to collapse with every new ounce of pressure.

*Why didn't I leave after that last guy?* she thought. *Then again, maybe this guy will turn into a new client.*

She had done these marketing days at the fitness center a few times now…it had been Linsey's idea. She wasn't sure if it was doing any good, but she always felt better for having tried something. Maybe today would yield a new client…maybe this guy. The thought of trying to work into this man's muscles on a regular basis seemed to send a panic down her limbs because her left fingers gave out for a brief second. She quickly recovered and pressed down his left shoulder with both hands, willing them to stay strong.

"So," she forced herself to say through the fog of her pain, "do you come here after work, or…" She let her question trail off.

"This is my work!" he said with gusto.

"Really?"

"I'm a personal trainer."

"Ah ha." Christina said with a nod. No surprise there.

"Gotta make sure I stay on top of my body if I expect people to trust me with theirs."

Christina nodded even though he couldn't see her.

"You come here to get some publicity…I walk around with a well-trained body as my publicity."

Christina tried not to laugh. "Do you enjoy your job?"

"Oh yeah! There's nothing better than working out, putting your energy into a challenge and seeing tangible results in your body."

Christina let a "yeah" slip from her lips, but her mind was sinking under the weight of that statement, like it was a mental barbell loaded with too much information. The idea of challenging her body was so foreign to her these days. She could remember what it was like to enjoy exercising, back in her early twenties. But apparently, twenty five was her middle age, because she just couldn't do it anymore.

A couple of women burst through the front doors, water bottles in hand, bags slung over their strong shoulders, legs ripply under their shorts. Their laughter filled the lobby like an edict. They looked to be in their mid-50s. Christina watched them check in at the desk, make the attendant laugh, then almost skip through the gym doors.

The man under her fingers was talking. "How long you been doing this?"

"Um, well, I've had my own practice for about a year, but I've been doing massage for three years now."

"You like it?"

"Yeah, I do. I like being able to help people feel healthy and well." If only I could do it for myself.

She glanced at her watch when her wrist was positioned towards her. 8 minutes. He probably wouldn't notice if I stopped two minutes early. But if he did notice, he probably wouldn't ever want to come to me again. She forced herself to press into another two minutes. By now, her head was throbbing.

"There you go," she said cheerily, stepping back so he could stand.

"Awesome. Thanks," he said tossing his head side to side. "Ah, that's nice."

Christina grabbed one of the coupons Linsey had helped her make. "Here, this is a coupon you can use if you come see me in my clinic. 10 percent off your first visit."

"Cool. I'll keep that in mind." He grinned at her, the shine of his perfect white teeth striking Christina much like his energy level did... shocking. "Well, good luck to ya. I hope you get hordes of clients from this."

But not you? Christina guessed with resignation.

He shook her hand and walked away on the balls of his feet.

Christina quickly collapsed her massage chair before she made eye contact with any of the other people starting to flood through the lobby. The end-of-the-work-day crowd. This was exactly when Christina should be offering free massages... but she just couldn't do any more. She grabbed her stuff and toted it out to her blue Ford Escape. She got behind the wheel and briefly laid her head against the steering wheel. She was in position for someone to give her a neck massage. But there was no one.

The pulsing of her achy heart seemed to be sending the pain directly up to her head. *Lord what's wrong with me? Get a grip Christina!* She blinked extra hard, turned the key and drove off.

•  •  •  •  •  •  •  •  •

Christina walked in the front door and shouted, "Don't!"

"You don't!" Linsey was kneeling on the floor, her left hand holding up her body while her right hand vigorously rubbed circles on the linoleum with a rag. A bucket of gently rocking brown water sat next to her.

"Oh Linsey," Christina said, gently thumping her throbbing head with the palm of her hand, "I was going to get to it. I swear."

Linsey looked up, her face flushed, strands of her brown hair falling out her ponytail and sticking to her moist cheeks. "It's okay Christina. I got it." Her face wasn't mad, just tired.

"I'm so sorry Linsey. I know you asked me to do it awhile ago. I just couldn't find time...or at least, a time when I wasn't tired...to do it." Christina sat down in a chair at the dining room table, leaning her head against her hand, thoroughly frustrated with herself.

"Christina, I said it's okay." Linsey brushed against the grime in the corner of the kitchen. She swooped the dirty rag up into the air with a flourish and tossed it into the bucket. "There. All done."

Christina sighed heavily. "It's the one chore I do around here...and I just can't seem to handle it."

Linsey stood up slowly pressing her hands into her low back and arching backward, groaning up at the ceiling. Then she grabbed the bucket, tiptoed to the sink, and emptied it. "Christina, I know you're stressed, and you've been getting a lot of your headaches. I can help you carry your load until you feel better."

"Linsey, you're carrying all the load...mine and yours."

"Eh..." Linsey shrugged. "I can handle it." She tiptoed over to the carpeted sitting room, combing her loose hairs up into a fresh ponytail. "Now, let's go to Costco."

Christina sighed. "I wish I could Linsey. But I'm sooo tired."

"Oh no you don't! You're not napping on me again." Linsey's hands went to her hips. "Come on. Please?"

"I can't. I wouldn't be any fun anyway."

"You're always fun to me Teena," Linsey said through a corny smile.

"Ahhhh! Geeee!" Christina feigned.

"I'll buy you a coffee on the way."

"I can't," Christina said sorrowfully. "I'm sorry I'm so lame."

"Oh man!" Linsey whined. She disappeared into her room, thumping dresser drawers and shoes onto the floor.

"Oh man!" Christina copied. She had heard that from Linsey so often lately. It felt horrible to be so disappointing to her best friend. "Why doesn't Robbie go with you?" She got up from the table and, with careful steps on the damp floor, popped her rice pack into the microwave.

"He's working late tonight," Linsey called from her room.

"I could go this weekend...if you wait."

"We seriously need toilet paper Teeners. Like, ASAP." Linsey appeared in the room again, fresh and perky, not a hint of dirty floor anywhere on her person. "Unless you want me to just go grab some leaves off the tree in the backyard? Would you prefer that?"

Christina scowled. "Yeah, that sounds great." Her mind briefly flitted to the exorbitant amount of money that they would inevitably spend at Costco. She wanted to contribute to things like toilet paper...she just didn't have any money. She never had any money! She wondered what a leaf would actually feel like. She retrieved the rice pack from the beeping microwave. She threw it around her neck and lay down on the couch.

"Besides, I wanted to get some supplies for the party on Friday."

"Oh yeah, Robbie's birthday party. I forgot." Christina felt a wave of exhaustion pull her down like gravity at the thought of another one of their infamous parties. She used to love them. Linsey always came up with such great themes: Runway Model, Worst Prom Dress, Hollywood Red Carpet, 80's Rock Bands. And the food, the drinks, the music, the games, the campfires. They were great. They really were.

Or they used to be...back when Christina had energy.

"By the way, bad news..."

"What?" Christina didn't open her eyes.

"You know that Wesley guy... Wesley Ohen...bowling..."

"Yeah." Now Christina did open her eyes. "The new guy you're trying to set me up with?" Linsey was always trying to set Christina up.

"That's the one. Well, he agreed to go bowling with Robbie and me tomorrow night."

"Really?" Now Christina lifted her head.

"And he's bringing his new girlfriend," Linsey said, crinkling her nose.

"Oh," Christina said, dropping her head back onto the pillow.

"So, I guess you're not coming," Linsey's voice was full of pity and irritation.

"Guess not." The gravitational pull was back.

"I'm sorry Tuh! I guess he just started seeing some 19-year-old girl."

"19!?"

"That's what I thought. I mean, 'Are you for real?'" Linsey threw her purse over her shoulder. "Come on... come with me and we'll rage about it together."

"Linsey, I can't."

Linsey looked at Christina with clear disappointment. "All right. Have a nice naaaaap," she said with a mixture of motherliness and sarcasm.

"Okay-dokey," Christina said, her eyes closed.

Linsey was barely out the door before the blanket of fatigue pulled up over Christina's consciousness, and the world receded into darkness.

. . . . . . . .

Friday night fellowship, The Way. A thousand young people, Christina's age...all fired up for Jesus.

Christina had been crying at these gathering for the last several weeks now. She couldn't seem to make it through a worship set without all her uncertainties and fears pouring out through her tear ducts.

Tonight was no different. She wiped her drippy nose with the tissues she had learned to start bringing to The Way.

Pastor John Mark was talking. Christina kept her head bowed, her warm watery eyes scanning the book of Psalms.

She was on Psalm 91:

> "He who dwells in the shelter of the Most High
>   will rest in the shadow of the Almighty.
> I will say of the Lord, "He is my refuge and
>     my fortress,
>   my God, in whom I trust."
>
> Surely he will save you from the fowler's snare
>   and from the deadly pestilence.
> He will cover you with his feathers,
>   and under his wings you will find refuge;
>   His faithfulness will be your shield and
>     rampart.
> You will not fear the terror of night,
>   nor the arrow that flies by day,
> nor the pestilence that stalks in the darkness,
>   nor the plague that destroys at midday.
> A thousand may fall at your side,
>   ten thousand at your right hand,
>   but it will not come near you.
> You will only observe with your eyes
>   and see the punishment of the wicked.

If you make the Most High your dwelling –
    even the Lord who is my refuge –
then no harm will befall you,
    no disaster will come near your tent.
For he will command his angels concerning you
    to guard you in all your ways;
they will lift you up in their hands,
    so that you will not strike your foot against a
      stone.
You will tread upon the lion and the cobra;
    you will trample the great lion and the
      serpent."

Christina sighed. *Yes Lord. You trample the lies, the fears, the despair.*

*Will you follow Me Christina?*

She read on, unconsciously hearing the Lord talking about her in His words:

"Because she loves Me," says the Lord, "I will
    rescue her;
I will protect her, for she acknowledges my
    name.
She will call upon Me and I will answer her;
    I will be with her in trouble,
    I will deliver her and honor her.
With long life will I satisfy her
    And show her my sal*vation.*"

*Will you follow Me Christina?*
And then the Lord's words came directly at her:

"Because you love me," says the Lord, "I will
    rescue you;
I will protect you, for you acknowledge my
    name.
You will call upon me, and I will answer you;
    I will be with you in trouble,
    I will deliver you and honor you.
With long life will I satisfy you

and show you my salvation."

*Will you follow Me Christina?*
The tears were flowing heavily now.
*Yes, Lord! I trust You! I will follow You, wherever You lead me!*

Unlike the many other tears shed over this summer, on this night, they cleansed instead of seared.

. . . . . . . . .

It was a glorious July weekend.

Christina was with her high school girls, on a rafting trip. The headaches had mercifully stayed away for the weekend. Christina had been able to do the rafting, do the playing, do the high-school-girl thing without very much pain at all. It was such a blessing.

On the last night, thirty high school girls sat around a circle of lanterns and flashlights meant to stand in for the banned campfire. The darkness of the summer night formed a warm blanket around the perimeter of the group, with a hazy yellow circle of light linking them together in an orb of youth and potential.

Christina was waiting for a quiet moment to speak. She was the lesson tonight. Despite her aversion to mass attention, this little talk in front of her high schoolers was a breeze. They were her girls...they were her friends. With a different audience, an audience of strangers, this would have been debilitating.

Across the circle, Linsey gave Christina a nod and an encouraging smile.

"Okay ladies, let's quiet down and we'll do a little chatting," Christina said. The girls didn't quiet down easily...they were teenage girls after all.

"Ladies," Christina tried again, her quiet, low voice doing little to penetrate the high-pitched chatter of the teenagers.

"Hello!" Linsey shouted. The girls started to quiet down. "Christina is going to share with us tonight. Let's give her some quiet."

"Thanks. I know you guys have lots of important things to discuss amongst yourselves," Christina said teasingly, "but if I could just have a few minutes, then you can go back to your conversations."

The girls smiled at her. Christina dug an elbow into the girls on her right and left.

"All right. So, I'm just going to share a little bit about what God has been doing in my life this last year, and then we can talk about it. And you guys know that I'm not a big fan of talking in front of people, even people I love like you guys, so you'll just have to bear with me if I get off track, or start rambling."

All eyes were on her. Christina slipped her sandals off, tapped them against each other and brushed off the bottoms of her feet.

"And when I get nervous about talking in front of people, my buns tingle, and they're tingling something fierce right now."

The girls squealed loudly. Christina chuckled with them as they teased her about her tingly behind.

When the laughter receded, Christina sighed. "Okay. Let's start then."

"Wait, let's pray for Christina first," Linsey interjected. "Would anybody like to pray for her?"

A girl named Kelsey volunteered to pray over Christina. As Kelsey prayed, Christina kept an eye open and scanned the down-turned faces of her girls. They all bore the stain of sunshine on shiny brown faces. Their hair was a bit ragged from the day of play, their eyes rather droopy from a physically and emotionally exhilarating weekend. They looked so pure out here in the wilderness.

At Kelsey's 'amen' the girls looked up to see Christina looking at them. Sweet smiles were exchanged, and Christina silently prayed that God would get through to each and every one of them.

"Thanks Kelsey. So, God has been doing a lot in me this past year. It's actually been a very challenging last few months. Some of you know some of these things already, but I'll just outline them all again. As you know, I just ended a relationship with someone."

The girls' lower lips protruded at the reminder that two people they really liked were no longer together.

"Which was a good thing, but hard nonetheless. I've also been a bit stressed about money lately. I've been trying to start my own massage business, build up a clientele and what-not. And I'm not too great at selling myself and creating a successful business, so I have been struggling financially for quite some time…which has been really hard for my pride."

The faces looking back at her were starting to take on pained looks as Christina shared her struggles. It made Christina's heart melt to see that these girls really cared about her.

"And then, on a physical level, I haven't been feeling very good for a long time now, probably from all the stress I've been feeling about those other areas of my life. I've gotten headaches throughout my whole life, but they seem to have jumped up a serious notch lately. Sometimes I have to just stand around in my bedroom early in the morning until they go away. I also get pains in my neck that can make it difficult to do my job. It's kind of a catch-22. I'm stressed about my job, so my neck and head hurt, which make it even harder to do my job. Plus, I get really tired throughout the day. Sometimes I just have to take a nap, I feel so fatigued...like I have nothing left to give. Which makes me feel like a pretty big loser when my business is failing, I'm in debt, and I'm just laying around in my house sleeping the day away. So I get stressed even more, and feel more tired, which makes my head hurt again."

Now the girls looked depressed.

"I'm not sharing this with you guys to get pity, or to make you feel bad or anything. You all look pretty bummed right now." Christina gave an encouraging laugh to lighten the mood. The girls ran hands over their faces, chuckled, but still looked sadly at her.

"I'm actually telling you this because God has been using all this stuff to teach me a really valuable lesson, one that I hope you guys have learned by now, or will learn soon, even though I don't wish pain on you in any way for you to learn it.

"So, I was struggling in three areas of my life: relationships, finances, and health. And oftentimes, those are three things that people will cling to in life, to make them feel okay, to give them a sense of security. And slowly, but quite clearly, those three things were stripped away from me. My relationship ended, I had no money, and I felt terrible physically. So one by one God would bring one of those things before me and ask me if I would surrender it to Him. He would say, 'Okay Christina, if that's the last relationship you'll ever have...if you spend the rest of your life alone, is that something that you'd be okay with?' And I had to get to the point where I was like, "Yes, Lord, of course. I couldn't want anything else Lord. You would be enough." It took a while to get there you know.

"And then He brought the next one to me. He said, "If you're going to struggle for the rest of your life with finances...if you have to live from paycheck to paycheck, sometimes even unsure of where the next one will come from, will that be okay with you? Will I be enough for you? Can you rely on Me to get you through that? Not just to get through it, but to live with joy through it?" And I was like, "Yes Lord, I can do that. I can rely on You to provide. You are enough. I will have joy in You.'

"And then God said, "Christina if you are going to have these headaches for the rest of your life, can you live with joy…can you be content with Me?" And, you know, that's pretty hard for me, because it's hard to imagine living the rest of my life feeling this way, but I've just had to get to the point where I can say to the Lord, "Yes Lord, I will be content with that. I will not be angry at You for my situation. I will live with joy through that."

"So all those things I've slowly had to let go of. And it wasn't a one time thing, and it's probably not necessarily a done deal. I'll have to continue surrendering each of those areas of my life…sometimes daily. But this is the life that God has given me, and why should I be upset that it hasn't necessarily turned out the way that I hoped it would. No one ever said life was going to be easy. God never promised that. He just says that He will walk through it with us, and His strength will be enough. So often we think that the circumstances of our life tell us how God is working. What I've been learning is that God's goodness is not determined by my circumstances. He's not good only if my pain goes away. He's not good only if I'm secure in a relationship. He's not good only if I have enough money. He's just good. So often our joy is dictated by things in our life. If only this and this and this… then I'd be happy. I've just had to get to the spot where I have to be happy and I have to be joyful through anything. And I am. And it's freeing to be able to just live with joy."

The girls stared wordlessly at her, their brows creased. Christina shifted on the sand. She made eye contact with each girl.

"My prayer for each of you is that you would be able to live your lives with joy. A joy that is not affected by your circumstances. A joy that doesn't exist because your expectations have all been met. Because, you know, bad things happen in life…sometimes we don't get what we expect, what we think we deserve. But God is a loving God. Our joy can come from His love. He loves each of us dearly… He knows us intimately, even knowing the number of hairs on our heads. The Bible says we are each more precious to Him than the lilies of the field, or the birds in the sky. And God loves the single poor girl," she raised her palms and tapped her chest, "as much as He does the secure, married, successful girl."

A couple heads nodded.

Christina smiled widely. "Now my buns are tingling, almost to numbness...but it's not from nerves. It's because I need to stand up. Come on join me." And, grabbing the arms of the girls on either side of her, Christina stood up and kicked her feet in the soft dirt around the fire; a dance of joy in the wilderness, because she was ready...for wherever God led her next.

# Staff in Hand

*Don't wish your storm away, but look for the power of God in it.*
*Love,*

*Christina*

"You again," Pharaoh said in a bored tone, not even rising from his throne. "Back to increase the workload of your people?" The people in the room chuckled.

Aaron stood tall and declared, "The God of the Hebrews says, 'Let my people go.'"

Moses prayed for the Lord's peace...that peace he had known when he had decided God would be enough for him.

Pharaoh leaned forward in his seat. "This god, how do I know he is who he says he is? Prove yourselves, and prove him to me. Perform a sign."

Aaron glanced over at Moses, who gave the slightest of nods so as not to draw any attention upon himself.

Aaron took the staff of the Lord from Moses and held it over his head. "Behold, the power of the Lord."

He tossed the staff onto the marble floor. It lay there for a moment. Then it filled with life. It became flexible and began to quiver. An "S" shape emerged from the straight line of wood; the knuckle at the handle formed a pair of beady eyes. A tongue licked out from the end.

Pharaoh rose quickly from his throne. The Cobra of Egypt looked down at the cobra of the Lord. Pharaoh was speechless.

Moses felt a jolt of joy in his belly as he watched the staring match.

Thank you Lord, Moses said at the apparent defeat he detected in Pharaoh's eyes.

But Pharaoh, never taking his eyes off the creature on the floor, flicked his hand at two men who stood coldly in the corner of the room. They stepped forward, staying out of the cobra's striking distance.

They too lifted their staffs. The muttered some unintelligible words, then threw their sticks to the ground. Immediately, two more snakes appeared, these ones Egyptian asps.

Moses gasped. Pharaoh's face turned smug.

*Lord?*

The snakes hissed at each other, slithering circles of provocation on the stones. Moses felt a swirling within his spirit as doubt lunged and spat at his faith.

Pharaoh sounded out a loud derisive laugh.

"This God of yours is not so special, is he?" he asked, putting contempt on the word 'god.'

Aaron said nothing, so neither did Moses.

*Lord? What is this?*

*Moses, will you follow Me? No matter what Pharaoh throws before you?*

*Yes, Lord. I will follow You no matter what.*

The snakes continued their dances of assertion. And then, in one swift motion, the cobra lunged at one of the Egyptian snakes. Ignoring the bites of the other, the Lord's creature swallowed one asp whole. Without waiting, the cobra turned on the other of the magician's snakes and also took it down with one decisive gulp. It then took a moment to circle its territory, its belly distended and lumpy.

Moses gulped in revulsion, but again felt a jolt of divine joy in his belly.

*Yes Lord.*

74

Pharaoh's mouth hung slightly open, his eyes bulging as he stared at the cobra. Then he turned his stare onto Moses and Aaron, his eyes turning to black beady stones. "Get out of my sight!" he shouted.

Moses stepped forward, approaching the cobra with boldness. He grabbed the serpent by the tail. The whole room gasped.

The snake twisted and turned in Moses' hand, but it did not strike at him. And after a few moments of 'God-be-glorified', the life faded from the stream-lined body of the serpent, and it hardened in Moses's hand. The knuckle returned where the head had been. Moses turned the staff right side up, and gripped it tightly in his hand. He looked up into the astonished eyes of the Serpent of Egypt and strode out of the room, Aaron close at his heels.

*I will follow You Lord.*

# September, 2007

Christina had nine days....nine days between her smiling and nodding to Dr. Crowley on Wednesday, and the open brain surgery she was scheduled to have at Emmanuel Hospital on Friday, September 21st, 2007.

During those nine days, information came to her and her family in spurts. They had another appointment with Dr. Crowley and met Dr. Vincent, who would be performing the angiogram the day before her surgery.

The prayer around the house and Christina's spiritual neighborhood was that the tumor would be benign: simply a confused, harmless clump of cells, growing in an inappropriate place. They were hoping for a low level meningioma... simple to remove: scoop out, fold in, staple up, recover from.

Tumors in the gray matter of the brain, the thinking part, would be more challenging...both to get out, and to the life of the patient. There are many of these kinds, and they all act differently. Christina and her family were having to process the possibility that her tumor could be aggressive, the type that would start growing back the day after her surgery, and lead to death very quickly.

When facing Death, some families take comfort in avoidance. Fear of Death causes these families to pull the shades and pass through the ordeal similar to how one afraid of flying might pass a plane ride: fingers gripping the seats, eyes closed, praying frantically, refusing to look out the window at the beauty around them. The choice to ignore and deny Death's nearness causes each person to pull a coat of protection around him/herself so as to ignore the painful Truth of fragility. Consequentially, each person is left alone and cold, covered in fear.

Other families take to the presence of Death in the family like a dog to its vomit: sickened by its presence, but choosing to devour its bitter and sad reality over and over again, passing up the bowl of fresh food next to them because they can't take their eyes off of it. In these families, Death becomes the VIP and all individuals fall to the wayside, lost in the shadow of the visitor.

Christina and her family took neither approach. Death was clearly acknowledged in their conversations. But it never overshadowed the joy of each and every day that Christina had; days spent with the people she loved, doing the things she loved, saying the things that needed to be said. Christina's transparency even led to a similar openness in others; for it's difficult to have a conversation with a person who may not be around in a few days and not feel the delicacy of one's own life as well. Conversations were rich; love was affirmed; people were real. The shadow of Death can actually be quite illuminating, when traversed with the Father of Light.

Christina and her supporters passed that week in Linsey and Christina's house on Pettygrove Lane with joy, with peace. They dubbed the place "The House of Peace." And that was not a willing-it-to-be-so nomenclature... like naming your daughter Chastity. This was an actual House of Peace. The peace of God was real and pervasive to all who came into contact with Christina and her family. Friends and family would come needing to see Christina, carrying their agitation and distress like a millstone around their necks. But when they walked through those doors, they walked into a bubble of peace, where the Lord's grace and providence shielded them from the lacerating reality of a broken world. They would see Christina's smiling face, see her do her 'old lady' impression, hear her use The Voice, join her laughter...they would see her living, not just alive. And they would watch Doug and JoDee love their daughter, as always...appreciating her and doting on her, as always. Things were strangely normal. That was a product of the Peace of God. There were moments of course, of sobriety...of sorrow at the possibilities. But they were never oppressive and they didn't usually stay for very long.

The peace that passes understanding was present and felt, even if inexplicably so.

· · · · · · · · ·

"I really like this one," Christina said, holding up the brown beanie. She put it on her head, shoving her full brown hair up under its cloth to mimic the look she would have in just a few days. She examined her face in the visor mirror. Her neck looked so small without her hair laying down on it.

"Yeah, I think that's my favorite," JoDee said, glancing over at Christina from the driver's seat.

"I like the red one," Tammy chimed in from the back. Tammy Hansen was one of JoDee's oldest and best friends. Tammy and her husband Dave had canceled all their life plans and headed to Portland once they heard of Christina's situation. They had known Christina her whole life, even acting as a second set of parents to Doug and JoDee's kids. Having two boys themselves, the Hansens had naturally taken to Christina as a daughter they did not have.

"This one?" Christina asked, donning the red one.

"Yeah. It's your color."

"My color huh?" Christina continued to study her face in the mirror, imagining how she would look after surgery next week. It was an unsettling thought that her face would be the only thing for people to look at when they interacted with her. Being a bald girl would be unusual, of course, but it wasn't just that... there's security to be found in your hair: its sheen, its style, its motion. It deflected attention from your face...from you. Christina would feel bare in more ways than one after next week.

"Did I already tell you that Jesse and Kristin got their flight finalized?" JoDee asked.

"No. When will they be here?"

"They fly in Saturday afternoon. They'll fly out again Monday morning."

"That's so great of them to come out." Christina's brother and sister-in-law lived in Montana. They had busy lives, and for them to make a quick trip out to Oregon was a very touching gesture. Christina knew this whole thing had upset her brother a lot...she knew he just needed to set his eyes on his little sister.

"How you doing Christina? How's your energy?" JoDee asked.

"Great! Thanks to the tumor pill."

"It's quite the wonder drug isn't it?" Tammy said.

"Yeah. It feels so good to be normal again... to be able to go through a day without needing a nap." Christina packed the beanies away. "Although it did keep me up a bit last night."

"Yeah, well the doctor warned you it might do that."

"Speaking of last night...that church service was fabulous!" Tammy said. "Your church is so wonderful Christina!"

"I know. They really are."

"The elders didn't just pray over you," JoDee said, "they probed. They wanted to know everything. They really care about you."

Christina nodded soberly at the reality of people caring.

"And the meal list!" JoDee continued. "Sooo wonderful!"

"I know. I know."

The hard part of last night's service for Christina had been trying to comfort her high school girls. Christina had been receiving hugs and scripture verses from friends and church elders when one of the elder's wives had pointed Christina toward a group of young girls crying in the corner of the sanctuary.

"I think they need to talk to you," the woman had whispered.

Christina wiped some tears from her own eyes and sauntered over to the teenagers. They all needed to hug her, see her, hear her assurances that her faith in the Lord was as sure as ever. They were unaccustomed to such severe reminders of life's frailty. Christina reminded them of the talk she had given on the rafting trip. She herself was thinking about it a lot these days. The Lord had led her through the refiner's fire this summer, drawing ever nearer to her little soul, refurbishing her, mending her, preparing her.

*I will follow You Lord.*

"Should we go to the computer store next?" JoDee asked.

Christina looked into the back seat where Tammy gave her a knowing look.

"Could we swing by Starbucks sometime during our errands?" Christina asked, suppressing a smile.

"Of course," JoDee said. "Anything for little Christina. Isn't there one off the highway up here?"

"Yeah."

"Do you want to go to that one, or wait 'til after the computer store?"

Christina glanced surreptitiously into the backseat where Tammy mouthed the words, 'Later is fine.'

"Oh, later is fine," Christina said, a smile creeping across her face.

JoDee's eyes flitted to the rearview mirror and then back to the road. She looked over at Christina, to the mirror, back to the road. "Tammy! Christina! What's going on? Are you the one who wants a latte?" she yelled at the rearview mirror, a laugh cracking her accusation.

Tammy dissolved into guilty laughter. "I made her ask you. I knew you wouldn't refuse her request."

JoDee shook her head. "Tammy, I wouldn't have refused your request either."

"I know. But I didn't want to be the reason we stopped."

"So you made Christina be the reason?"

"I'm happy to be the reason," Christina chimed in over the peals of laughter.

It felt so good to laugh. It was evidence that God did indeed walk with them through the valley of the shadow of death.

. . . . . . . . .

On September 20th, Christina woke clear-headed and alert.

She lay in bed looking at the perfect sunny day outside. This was it...this was the day. A girl who had never spent a night in a hospital was about to sign up for open-brain surgery. Today she would have an angiogram, spend the night in ICU, and have her long surgery tomorrow.

*Okay Lord. This is it.*

Christina sighed. She knew this day absolutely must start in prayer. She just wasn't sure what to pray.

*Thank You for all You've given me Lord. Thank You for this peaceful week. It was such a blessing. I'm ready Lord...go before me. Take care of my family Lord. Please, give them Your peace.*

As always, tears came when Christina thought of her family.

*Be with them Lord, even if I will not be.*

Christina wiped away a rolling drop of salty acceptance.

She stared around her room. It was decorated with her life. A guitar sat in its stand, always waiting for her to pick it up and learn its craft. Through the open doors of her closet, she could see her violin case, a rarely opened treasure of her youth. Pictures lined her walls and rested on the surfaces of her furniture. So many friends, arms draped over her shoulders. Some of the faces had sweet smiles, some had open mouths caught mid-laugh, some had silly looks in moments of goofiness. All were happy faces. If she listened carefully, she could hear their laughter echoing off the walls of the life she had constructed.

What would her life be like after this morning? Would she have life? Would she be the same? What would the future be like if she had a physical disability? Would her left leg obey her anymore after today? Would she walk in circles the rest of her life? What if a week from now, Christina the body came home, but Christina the girl was gone forever? What if she turned into a cursing, angry, unhappy frump?

More drops into her well of acceptance.

80

*Lord, You are enough. I will go where You lead me. Just let the life I lead from this day forward bring You glory.*

She wiped her face, patted her cheeks and took some big breaths. Always wanting to shield her family from the heaviness to which she occasionally fell victim, Christina made sure to erase its evidence before leaving her room.

She headed to the bathroom to shower…her last one for a few days. As she washed her hair with the hospital-supplied antibacterial shampoo, she caressed her brown locks lovingly, sadly. She felt a heat in her eyes again.

*It's just hair Christina!* she chided herself.

After drying off and dressing, she blow-dried her hair, watching every strand slowly go from dark brown to light brown. Then she stared at herself for a moment before pulling her hair back away from her face. There was her thin neck again…there was her stark face…there was Christina.

She released her ponytail. Each strand of hair elbowed for room among its million siblings, finally settling into restful repose. Christina felt a camaraderie with each little hair and the role they had played in her life. She quietly said a collective goodbye to them. The One who knew each and every strand on her head would take care of them…and her.

The house smelled of coffee. Dave Hansen was busy in the kitchen making his killer lattes: foamy and filling.

"Ah man!" Christina cried as she entered the kitchen. "Y'all are having lattes?"

Her favorite people in the world all looked at her with apologetic smiles.

"Dave's lattes to boot!" Christina bumped her hip against Linsey's shoulder.

"Sorry Christina," her dad sighed.

"I promise you, I'll make you the best latte ever once you're back," barista Dave said from his post at the latte machine.

"…once you're back." Christina thought on that phrase.

"What do you need this morning?" Linsey asked, ready to jump into action.

"Well, since I can't eat, I guess I'll just watch you all eat," Christina joked, "and make you feel bad about it." She sat down at the table, placed her chin in her hand and, leaning forward, stared directly at Tammy and her cup of joe.

"Noooo," Tammy said, over her cup.

"I'm kidding. I'll just chill…maybe take a walk."

"We don't actually have that long," JoDee said looking at her watch. "We should probably leave no later than 11 am."

"I'm ready, whenever," Christina said.

. . . . . . . . .

Christina walked into the hospital flanked on either side by JoDee and Doug, Linsey, Dave and Tammy Hansen. The troupe strode down halls, pushed open doors, and walked right into Christina's future in a V-formation. Christina was not alone.

They checked in at the day surgery desk. Christina stared through her funktified eyeballs at the questions on the forms she was given:

"What is your medical issue?'

She wrote: Brain tumor.

"What have you done for this issue?"

Christina wrote: Ibuprofen, Tylenol, physical therapy, massage… nothing's helped. ☺

The entourage walked back with her to the holding room. They all wanted to be with her every second that they could.

A nurse came into the room, her eyes touching on every face in the crowded space.

"Well hello," she said in a friendly way.

Christina said "Hello" for all of them.

"You're Christina?" the nurse asked, with an understanding look.

"That's me," Christina said with a smile.

The nurse's face flickered. "Well, I'm Heather, and I'm here to make sure you'll be prepped and ready for your cerebral angiogram today."

"Great!" Christina said.

Heather looked confused at Christina's mood. "Do you have any questions?" she asked, poking at the source of that confusion.

Christina shook her head, but JoDee piped in. "Are we going to see Dr. Vincent before the surgery?"

Heather wrapped the pressure cuff around Christina's arm. "I don't know if he's planning on coming in before the actual surgery, or if you'll just see him in the operating room when you get there."

JoDee pursed her lips. A mother wants to see the man who will poke holes in her daughter. Does he look alert? Did he get enough sleep? Did he wear glasses? Was his grip firm? Did he understand exactly who he had on his medical table?

"Could you explain real quick how an angiogram works?" Christina said, always plagued by ignorance.

"Sure." Heather went quiet for a moment, listening to the beats of Christina's arm. The room remained silent for her. She pulled off the earpiece and put the armband away. "Arteries don't show up on X-rays. So, in order to see what kind of blood flow your tumor has, a dye has to be injected into your carotid arteries," Heather pointed at the hint of blue lined down her neck, "and then the X-rays can show its movement."

"But you'll be going in through my hip?" Christina asked.

"That's correct. Angiograms are usually performed through the artery in your groin. They make a nick about the size of a pencil tip and then insert a catheter through it."

"And the catheter travels from the hip to the brain?" JoDee asked skeptically.

"That's right." Heather was patient with their questions. "The catheter is a very small hollow tube that travels..." she was running a finger from her hip up her torso, "...very cautiously," she smiled, "up through the circulatory system to the neck. The dye is released from there."

Every face in the room had a squeamish look.

"And aren't they hoping to cauterize some blood vessels too?" Dave asked.

"Yes, I think so." Heather grabbed her clipboard and flipped through a couple pages. "They're hoping to be able to cut off the flow of blood to the tumor. That would keep the bleeding down for surgery tomorrow."

"But they might not be able to cut off the blood flow?" JoDee pressed.

Heather waved a hand through the air. "Of course they don't know what they're dealing with. It could be a situation where the blood flow is not concise." She stopped, realizing that the family wanted details. "If it's a simple tumor, a benign one like a meningioma, the blood flow to it will be clear, easy to cut off. If the tumor is large and complicated, then the blood flow will be also. They will not be able to cauterize the blood vessels because of their size and extensive reach." She looked around to see if that was satisfactory.

Christina smiled, wanting to reassure Heather that it was okay...she didn't have to dwell on the bad possibilities.

Heather grabbed her materials and made as if to leave. "Today's procedure will make all those questions more clear." She stood, clipboard in hand, smile on her face. Then her eyes scanned the room again. "So, we'll need everyone to leave for a moment so Christina can get undressed."

A large pressure seared through Christina's empty stomach. How undressed?

Her family headed for the door. JoDee and Tammy lingered a little, JoDee's arm draped over her daughter's shoulder.

Heather was at the door too. "Now when I come back, you need to be wearing only that gown, okay Christina?"

And she was gone.

Christina turned to Tammy, the pressure deepening. "Ohhh man! I gotta take my panties off!"

Tammy turned to Christina, a chuckle seeping out, "Oh man!" she echoed.

JoDee gave Christina a sympathetic look.

It was not a surprise to Christina. Of course, with a tube traveling up to her brain from her hip, she would probably have to be bared for the procedure. Not a surprise...but unpleasant nonetheless.

"Oh man!" Christina said again.

"Christina," her mom said. "You'll be okay."

"I know, but...oh man!!"

"They're professionals Christina," Tammy said.

"I knooooow."

"We'll be back," JoDee said, walking toward the door. Her eyes rested on her daughter a moment, capturing the sight of Christina looking totally normal one more time.

Christina watched the door shut on her support. Not that she would want them here at this moment, but suddenly the cold loneliness of the room hit her. She started with her shirt. Then her pants. She made herself completely bare in the sterile hospital room, longing for the comfort of the life and people that were outside. She quickly donned the gown, trying to pinch it more tightly together then the strings managed to do. She noticed how pale and weak her skin looked in the lighting.

She scrambled onto the bed, pulling the blanket up to her

shoulders, feeling shivery and cold even though the room was plenty warm. The sheets were coarse and starchy against her skin. She realized she hadn't shaved her legs in a fair spell, and the stubble stuck to the thick fibers of the sheet.

The air around her hummed audibly. She couldn't figure out if it was the lights or some random machine that never silenced.

*Lord, are You there?*

The hum answered her.

*I know You're there Lord.*

The room hummed some more.

Then a knock on the door and Heather's smiley face peeked in. "You ready?" she asked, as if there was still a chance at privacy with her face already in the room.

"I'm ready," Christina said, grateful for a sound other than the hum. Heather stepped into the room in a flurry of rustling fabric and soft footfalls.

She shut the door behind her, but immediately another knock sounded on it, and JoDee's face peeked through. "Can we come in?"

Heather beckoned her in and five bodies crowded into the room again. Heather worked around them, arranging Christina's bed.

When Heather left, the group looked comfortably at each other.

Linsey, who was scanning her cell phone, asked, "Christina, could you do the rap?"

JoDee laughed immediately.

Christina laughed when the beat burst forth from the small speakers on Linsey's phone. The tinny sound somehow filled the room.

Christina reached down and grabbed the controller for the bed's height. She held it inches from her mouth like a microphone.

She busted it out, not too loud, for fear of drowning out the beat. Her rapping was soft, but the laughs of her audience were loud.

Heather walked into the room in the middle of the song, and the confusion appeared again. But it quickly melted into a humorous smile. She watched a minute, then left.

Her family clapped abundantly when she was finished.

· · · · · · · · ·

They sat around for several hours, waiting. The angiogram was supposed to start at 1:30 but, for reasons only known to the doctors, it was delayed.

Nurse Heather checked in on them frequently, always surprised by the lighthearted atmosphere in the room. At one point, she asked Christina how she was feeling.

"Okay," was Christina's response.

"Are you particularly nervous?" Heather asked.

"Well, I'm nervous," Christina said. "Who wouldn't be nervous about an upcoming brain surgery?"

"Because we can give you some Valium if you want."

Christina lit up. "Okay!"

"What?" JoDee asked.

"I mean, you don't really seem like you need it, but..." Heather continued.

"I've never had Valium," Christina said, ready to experience anything new on this day of firsts.

"I don't think you need any drugs, Christina," JoDee said with a smile.

Christina shrugged. "I mean, I don't need it, but I'm happy to try it."

Heather looked skeptical.

"It's not something to just try," Linsey said. "I think you're fine Teena."

Christina shrugged again.

"Well, if you find yourself getting really nervous, just let me know," Heather said and left.

"Okay. Thanks," Christina said.

Her family was grinning at her.

"'I'm happy to try it,'" JoDee mimicked.

"What? When else am I ever going to get to try Valium?"

"Hopefully never!" Tammy chimed in.

Just then, the phone in the room rang. With no nurse around to pick it up, Doug grabbed the receiver and said, "Hello."

The room watched him as he listened. Suddenly, his brow crinkled and he said, "No." Pause. "No, absolutely not."

Then he calmly set the phone back in its cradle.

"What was that about?" JoDee asked.

Doug looked amused. "They wanted to know if there was any chance that Christina was pregnant."

Every chin lowered and the room went quiet.

Finally Tammy burst out, "They asked the dad if the girl was pregnant?!"

Now every head fell back in a giant laugh.

"What nurse asks a father if his daughter is pregnant?" JoDee exclaimed.

Doug shrugged his shoulders, chuckling.

Christina chimed in, "What's he supposed to say, 'no... I mean... I don't think so... are you by any chance... uh... no.'"

They all laughed again.

"I figured it was safe to say 'no,'" Doug said innocently.

"Of course the answer is 'no,' it's just hilarious that they would ask you," Christina said again.

"'No.'" JoDee said, mimicking Doug's calm response to the bizarre phone call. "'No. Absolutely not.'"

They laughed again.

. . . . . . . . .

During the angiogram, JoDee sat alone in the hospital lobby eating a salad. Everyone expected the procedure to last 2-3 hours, so there was a scattering of family as they set out to accomplish tasks. Twenty minutes later, JoDee looked up to see Dr. Vincent walking towards her.

JoDee stood up, swallowing an unchewed bit of salad.

"This can't be good news," she said.

Dr. Vincent looked at her with consternation. "We were unable to cauterize the blood vessel that supplies the tumor. It turns out that the blood flow is very complex and tied into all the vessels that supply her brain with blood. If we tried to cut off the flow to the tumor, we would also be cutting off flow to her brain, which could result in brain damage."

JoDee felt her throat tightening. The taste of balsamic vinaigrette in her mouth was bitter and strong. Her head ached. She wiped her nose, furious at the cold she was developing.

"This means it's probably not a meningioma, correct?" she asked.

"No. It's not a meningioma," Dr. Vincent confirmed, looking sad.

JoDee nodded.

"On a positive note, we now have a fantastic vascular map for the surgery tomorrow. It will help Dr. Crowley immensely."

JoDee nodded again, trying to hold on to that 'positive note.'

"I'm sorry I don't have better news for you. Christina will be

87

in the ICU in a few minutes, and you'll be able to visit her there. Someone will come for you."

"Thank you," JoDee said weakly, watching Dr. Vincent stride away, his scrubs making swishing sounds in the lobby.

JoDee sank into the chair, tears forming. She stared at her salad. The lettuce sprigs were wilting under the dressing's acids.

She picked up the phone and called her friend Nancy Stack in Hawaii. She cried, "It's not a meningioma. That probably means it's cancerous."

"Nothing has changed," Nancy said firmly. "God is not surprised by this."

After receiving some severe comforting from Nancy, JoDee called Doug who was running errands. He was shocked.

Then she called the Hansens who were shopping with Linsey at Safeway. Tammy fell to her knees in the store.

Portland was the epicenter of a shocking turn of events for all who knew and loved Christina. Meanwhile, the recipient of that love was peacefully sleeping in the ICU.

. . . . . . . . .

Christina became aware of a loud beeping. She felt like she was riding on the rolling swells of the Puget Sound, with the clanging of a distant buoy the only thing keeping her near the shore. Then a voice flowed along the beeping cadences, bumping up against her senses, nudging her toward consciousness. The sounds grew more solid, more real.

Now there were two voices.

There were words.

The words were about her.

"She's here a bit sooner than we expected. The angiogram was short. They tried to cauterize the vessel that fed the tumor, but the blood flow was too large."

"Oooh, that's too bad. She's so young."

Christina lay with her eyes closed, listening. She must have already had the angiogram. She couldn't remember anything after her trip to the operating room where Dr. Vincent had greeted her.

Apparently the attempt to cut off the tumor's blood flow had not worked.

Christina was very groggy, but these thoughts were clear. The tumor was large…and bad. It was not a meningioma.

*Lord, thank You for Your love.*

• • • • • • • •

Sometimes, the earth takes a deep breath and adjusts itself. It's a slight movement to the earth; but it's an earthquake to the people above ground.

Sometimes, life takes a breath and makes a similar adjustment. Is God any less God because things happen that jolt us? Absolutely not. Can He step in and shield us from the breath of trouble? Of course. Does He have to? Of course not. Does His love and provision falter in the face of life's earthquakes? No way!

"Shall I accept good from God and not trouble?" Job asked.

Christina asked the same thing of herself many times throughout her journey, as she seemed to continually find herself diagnosed with the worse of two options. "Bad things are happening all over the world," she would say. "Why shouldn't they happen to me?" She wasn't angry. Sad often, confused sometimes, scared even…angry, no.

Not all people react that way when life sighs in their direction.

And that's okay.

• • • • • • • •

After her angiogram, Christina spent the night in ICU, receiving the best care possible, from the hospital staff and from Linsey. They snacked until the nurses cut them off from their salt and vinegar chips. They watched 'The Princess Bride' on Linsey's laptop, reciting their favorite lines with nurse Paddy when she would check on them. They fielded the many comments made about how young they were to be in this position.

They scoped out the prisoner in the room next to them…prisoner, in literal terms. Apparently, an inmate from one of the local prisons had taken something to give himself a seizure so that he could spend some time outside his walls. But his stay in the hospital mostly involved his being handcuffed to the bed, making strange and threatening noises. Christina and Linsey took it all in, wide-eyed.

89

. . . . . . . . .

That night, JoDee sat in a hotel room by herself. She was alone...for the first time since all of this had started. Doug was staying at Pettygrove Lane to be more available for the logistics of the next few days. Dave and Tammy were also at Pettygrove Lane, resting for tomorrow. JoDee's friend Kim was scheduled to arrive in a couple hours to be with JoDee through the night. But for now, JoDee was alone. It was 10 pm. She had just left Christina and Linsey at the hospital, chatting and eating chips.

JoDee sat in a chair in the corner of the room. Looking around, she could see a bouquet of flowers in the vase on the table, a box of chocolates on the bed's pillow, a note from Dave and Tammy who had left all these treats when they had gotten the room for her. The queen-sized bed with its tight flowered bedspread stretched across its surface, looked lonely in the dimly lit space. There was no noise except the movement of the air coming from the floor vent, air that tickled her bare ankles.

JoDee's journal lay closed in her lap on top of her Bible. She sat in the semi-darkness, every thought and emotion just barely under the surface of her self-control. Her body ached from the cold virus which was just peaking within her. She knew she should lie down and try to sleep, but she couldn't. The ache of her body and her soul was too great.

Tomorrow morning, her only daughter was going to go under a surgeon's knife. That knife would open up her head and probe within the very organ that made her daughter who she was. JoDee had been preparing emotionally and mentally for this moment from the time the possibility had arisen. But as the moment drew near, its enormity, its finality began to sink in. Today could be the last day of her life as a mother of two children. JoDee felt a sudden dearth of oxygen.

She breathed deeply and opened up her Bible to Isaiah 40:

"He tends His flock like a shepherd:
    He gathers the lambs in His arms
and carries them close to His heart;
    He gently leads those that have young.

He gives strength to the weary

90

and increases the power of the weak.
Even youths grow tired and weary,
  and young men stumble and fall;
But those who hope in the Lord
  will renew their strength.
They will soar on wings like eagles;
  they will run and not grow weary,
  they will walk and not be faint."


JoDee opened up her journal. She wrote: "Lord, my great hope for surgery tomorrow is that afterward I will get to see Christina in her right mind and fully functional. Whatever else comes from the procedure, Lord, we'll deal with that as it comes. But I don't want tomorrow morning to be goodbye to my daughter."

As she wrote, JoDee's eyes and nose flowed profusely.

She put her pen and Bible down and wiped furiously at her tears. She looked around the dark, lonely hotel room. She kept seeing images of her small, button-nosed little girl, chased away by images of Christina in a hospital gown, in pain.

"What am I doing here?" she asked herself. She sat up quickly. "Lord, what am I doing here?"

She picked up the phone and called Pastor Mike and Jan Jones, who were in a hotel nearby. They coordinated to get JoDee back to the hospital the moment Kim pulled into town.

Thus, at about midnight, JoDee took a deep calming breath outside of Christina's room in the ICU. She wasn't sure what she would find inside. Would her daughter be fine? Would she be depressed, unable to find the Lord in this night? Praying mightily, JoDee walked in. The girls had just wrapped up their viewing of "The Princess Bride." Both their eyes were heavy with fatigue and their lips were pickled from the chips. They were smiling, laughing even, and happy. JoDee told them she was just checking in one last time. Christina smiled brightly at her mother, attempting to pass her peacefulness on to her mother. JoDee said goodnight, blowing Christina a kiss so as not to subject her to nasty germs, and then carried her heavy heart out of the peaceful room. She led Kim to the waiting room and sat down.

Christina was clearly fine, bolstered by the distraction and love of her best friend. But was JoDee fine? She couldn't leave yet. She didn't want to be in Christina's room, passing on her worries and fears to her calm daughter. But she couldn't leave the building. She needed to be near, for now.

She and Kim lay down on the waiting room couches, each with their arms wrapped around their shoulders to unsuccessfully fend off the chill in the air. They dozed for about an hour. Then JoDee stood up, walked back to Christina's room where the lights were out and the faint hum of machines was the only sound. Linsey was curled up in the hard chair, asleep. Christina slept on her back, her head tilted to the side.

JoDee walked in and stood at the side of her daughter's bed. She studied that face, a face 25 years familiar, as if she were seeing it for the first time. It was beautiful. It was full of peace.

JoDee wept.

. . . . . . . . .

"Okay Kim," JoDee said, nudging her friend who was only halfway into a sleeping state. "We can go now."

Kim rubbed her eyes, stood up, and walked JoDee out to their car.

. . . . . . . . .

The nurses woke Christina at 6 in the morning to prep her for brain surgery.

As nurses bustled around her, Pastor Mike came in for a private session.

"How you feeling Christina?"

"I'm okay. I'm nervous, but I'm okay."

"Have you thought of the possibility of death Christina?" he asked, his eyes gentle.

"Yes I have," Christina said resolutely. "I've talked to God about it."

"Okay?" Pastor Mike said questioningly.

"I just want God to take care of my parents if I go." Christina's eyes glistened.

"He will."

"I know." She wiped her eyes. "As for me, the way I see it, if I go under anesthesia and then die…I just go to sleep and wake up to Jesus' face. What could be better?"

Pastor Mike smiled. "What could be better indeed?"

Shortly after, her parents walked into the room.

"All the elders from your church are in the lobby Christina," JoDee said.

"They're praying for you," Doug added.

"Wow," Christina said. "That's so great."

A cute male nurse named Jeff came in and shaved a few dime-shaped spots on her scalp where the electrodes would be placed.

"Why just the spots?" JoDee asked. "Isn't all the hair going to be coming off anyway?"

"Yeah," Christina said. "Just putting off the baldness for as long as possible?"

Jeff paused in his work to answer. "They'll shave your whole head in the operating room as part of their prep. These are just specific spots that need to be smooth as a baby's bottom."

"A baaaaaby's bottom?" Linsey squeaked in The Voice. "Teena's gotta baaaaaby's bottom scalp?"

"So sweeeeeet and smooth," Christina said. It felt good to laugh in the midst of the drama.

Jeff laughed with them.

. . . . . . . . .

Christina was wheeled on a gurney into the operating room, her parents on either side of her. There faces were calm, thoughtful.

"I love you Christina," they both said when they reached the doors of their separation.

"I love you guys," Christina said, releasing their hands as they stayed still and she rolled forward.

The nurses held open the door and Christina watched the metallic operating room and its inhabitants enter her life.

She got to hear all their names and duties. Dr. Crowley and his assistant Drew she already knew. She smiled at the nurses, orderlies, the anesthesiologist and technologist.

It was all very surreal. All these people staring at her, focused on her, intent on her. Did they see HER? Or just her tumor?

Christina pulled the warm blanket up tightly around her neck, like a turtle peeking out from her shell. The movement of the sheets prickled her stubbly legs.

She tried not to let the tidal wave of questions and emotions distort the peace of God she had been feeling. She was here with Him to take care of the problem that had taken up a coiled residence in her head.

She just prayed for her family.

…and there they were. Someone had let them back in to meet the hands that would find and fight the tumor. They stood there, vulnerable and anxious against the cold green of the room. A strong dose of reality in a world unknowable.

After a few minutes, goodbyes were constructed again. Christina watched her parents pass through the doors again, leaving her behind. But she could feel their prayers, as real as their corporeal bodies had been a moment before.

"We're going to take you back here," Drew said, wheeling Christina to a back room, "to prepare you for the procedure. We'll hook you up to a heart monitor and catheter. The IV will be in your neck. Apparently they weren't able to get it in your arm this morning."

"Too much muscle," Christina offered, flexing her biceps to prove her point.

"Absolutely! The muscle mass got in the way," Drew chuckled. "But you won't be aware of most of this stuff since you'll be given the gas right away."

"Happy gas?"

"Oh yeah. Real happy. And of course, once you're under, I'll be shaving your head."

"Oh boy!" Christina joked.

"I don't know if anyone's mentioned this to you yet, but I could just shave half your head if you'd prefer."

Christina chuckled. "Half my head?"

"Just an option," Drew said lamely. "…you could comb it over."

"Ha!" Christina couldn't contain a laugh that time. The echo-y room circulated the sound. "NO! No combovers!. That would be gross."

"It could be a new trend," Drew offered. "Girly-combovers."

"Yeah, that's me. I'm a trend-setter man. Introducing Christina Ahmann and the new girly combover. No…not okay. You just do what you gotta do. I'm prepared to lose it all."

"All right," Drew said with a smile. "I'll just try to make it all even for you."

"I trust you Drew. I'm sure you'll do a great job."

Drew smiled again.

The anesthesiologist descended upon her at that moment, a gas mask in his hands. "This will deliver the gas that will put you under. You'll feel a warmth, and then you'll just drift into a nice sleep." His voice lilted as if he was trying to send her calmly into that nice sleep.

"I sure could use a nice sleep. I'm pretty tired." Christina yawned, looking up into the chilly lights above her. The mask rested on her cheeks and chin.

"How are we going to know if the drugs are working on you?" Drew said. "You're so goofy."

"I don't know," Christina said, her voice muffled behind the mask. There was a sound from the mask, but no smell, no taste. "I guess when I pass out, you'll know it worked."

And she passed out...her last thoughts resting on the friendly chitchat of people she hardly knew, yet people who gave her a human touch to send her into God's plans for her future.

* * * * * * * * *

More sound waves were landing on the shores of Christina's consciousness. More crests and valleys of human voices, beeping out patterns Christina was starting to recognize through the darkness. More talking about her.

"She's so young."

"I know. She's 25."

"So sad."

Christina blinked against some eye crusties.

"Christina?" one of the voices said firmly.

Christina blinked lazily. She looked around the room. And then a message in her body woke her up very quickly. An enormous pressure was calling for attention in her lower abdomen.

"Can you hear me darlin'?" the voice was saying. A woman's face floated into Christina's sight, her eyebrows meeting in the middle of her forehead with concern.

"Yes," Christina said with a voice that had traveled over the rough stones of a dry desert stream.

"Do you know your name?"

"Christina."

"Good." The eyebrows released slightly.

"I really have to go to the bathroom," Christina croaked, trying to punctuate her words with an exclamation point.

The eyebrows joined up again. "Well...you have a catheter in darlin'. So...just... let it go."

Christina concentrated, feeling her own eyebrows visiting on her brow. The pressure was not abating. Any effort on Christina's part to 'just let it go,' only increased the discomfort.

"Um...I...can't," she said weakly, her efforts tiring her.

The nurse moved out of her line of sight. "Oh! My goodness! Well...that's no good!" There was a sound of rubber being pinched and pulled. "Let me just...There!"

Immediately, the pressure began to subside. "Ahh..." Christina couldn't keep herself from exclaiming at the relief.

"Is that better?" the face reappeared.

"Yes!"

"Good. How are you feeling?"

"I'm really thirsty," Christina said, her sandpaper tongue running across the waxy landscape of her lips.

The nurse quickly produced some ice chips and brought them to her mouth. "Here you go. You don't want to overdo it, so we'll just start with some ice chips." She gently placed them on Christina's tongue. The cool wetness bathed her mouth and throat in comfort.

"Thank you," she whispered, feeling fatigue set in again now that her immediate needs were met. Her eyelids were heavy, and she let them close again.

"You just rest darlin'," the voice said, riding the beeping sound waves.

. . . . . . . . .

Some time later, Christina was being wheeled from the recovery room to the ICU, where her many fans would be able to see her. Feeling tense at the bed's motion, Christina lay stiffly through the transfer. Then, a familiar sound hit her ears. It was a voice...Dave's voice.

"Hey," Christina said, her own voice suddenly strong.

At the end of the hall by the elevator, Christina saw Dave Hansen and Jan Jones standing together. There faces went weak with shock at the sight of her.

Christina lifted a hand off her bed. Dave hurried over and grabbed it, his eyes wet with heavy tears. Jan gave Christina's arm a quick pat. "I'll go tell everyone in the lobby," she said before hurrying away.

Dave walked alongside Christina, his weepy eyes saying everything his voice could not.

"Hey," Christina said again, a huge smile stuck on her face.

At the doors to the ICU, the nurses told Dave he would have to stay behind. He squeezed Christina's hand, softly saying, "We love you Christina."

Their hands parted and Christina passed through the door, leaving a weeping Dave alone in the hallway.

• • • • • • • • •

Christina woke again, her heart leaping with joy at the face before her.

JoDee's countenance was serene, peaceful. Putting her eyes to her daughter's face, whole and familiar, was enough for her in the moment. Christina could almost see her mother's prayers of gratitude to the Lord at that very moment.

JoDee wiped her nose.

"Hi Christina," she said softly.

Christina grinned broadly, her dry lips stretching tightly.

"Hi Christina," her father's voice came to her, quickly followed by his grinning face. He too looked at peace.

"You look beautiful." JoDee said, and Doug nodded.

Christina smiled.

On the other side of the bed, Pastor Mike stood, a big smile on his face.

Christina smiled at everyone, then said, "So...how did it go?"

JoDee studied her a moment. "Do you really want to know?"

"Yeah," Christina nodded.

"Well, the surgery went well. They got most of the tumor out. And..." JoDee paused, studying Christina again, "...it looks malignant."

The word hung in the room, its impact interrupted only by the sounds of the machines that took measurements of Christina's vitality. The beeps were loud and strong.

Christina nodded, knowing this moment would come. With the results of the angiogram yesterday and the nagging suspicion in her spirit, Christina had already prepared for this truth.

"Here we go then," she said.

JoDee looked at her intently. "My great desire was to still have my daughter at the end of this day." She put her hand on Christina's.

"God has answered my prayer."

Doug nodded.

"So, what do we do now?" Christina asked.

"Right now, you recover from surgery," JoDee said firmly.

"That's right," Doug echoed.

"They got most of the tumor though?" Christina asked, hungry for more information.

"That's what Dr. Crowley said. With the bulk of the tumor gone, you should be relatively free of those headaches now, and can get back to normal," JoDee said.

The word 'normal' hung in the room the way 'malignant' had a moment before. They all knew nothing would be 'normal' again.

A nurse came in to check Christina's vitals. Her parents made room for her.

"How are you feeling Christina?" the nurse asked.

"My head kind of hurts."

"Well, you did just have surgery on your head," the nurse said with a smile.

"It really hurts right here," she pointed to a spot on her temple, "and here," she pointed to the other side of her temple.

"Yes, well, that's where they screwed your head to the table," the nurse said gently.

Christina's mouth formed an "O" of understanding. Her parents and Pastor Mike grimaced.

"You know what's weird?" she said as the nurse gingerly checked the tube that penetrated Christina's skull to drain excess liquid from her brain.

Her parents looked at her questioningly.

"My head hurts, but it somehow feels really good too. Like, I have a headache, but not one of THOSE headaches."

Her parents nodded.

"It's like I've lost that intense pressure in my head." She beamed at the thought.

JoDee chuckled. "What kind of patient smiles after a long, grueling surgery on the brain?"

The nurse looked up. "I was wondering the same thing myself."

"Have you noticed something else Christina?" JoDee asked.

Christina looked around for a clue.

"You have something all over your head," Doug prompted.

Christina gingerly put a hand on her head, afraid of what she would find. She could feel her hair in her fingers. She could feel her **hair**!!! "I have hair!" she squealed.

"You have a full head of hair," JoDee said with a large smile.

"What happened?"

"I don't know. I guess Jeff, the guy who was shaving the dots on your head this morning, suggested that they just do a racing stripe where the incision would be and let you keep the rest. There's just a thin line down the side Christina. It won't even be noticeable once your hair lies normally on your head."

"That's pretty special Christina," Doug said.

"Yeah!" Christina was fondling her hair, trying to avoid the truly tender spots. It felt great to run her fingers through it. "So cool!"

They all enjoyed the hair-joy as the nurse finished up and left.

"Would you guys like to pray?" Pastor Mike asked. "Thank God for this moment, and pray for the moments to come?"

"Yes please," Christina said.

They prayed together.

Christina kept her eyes closed after the prayer, fatigue overtaking her. Her parents sat quietly, respecting her need to rest.

· · · · · · · · ·

The rest of that day was a bit of a blur to Christina. She drifted in and out of sleep and delirium. Her waking moments were weighed down by the tug of the drugs, pain and fatigue. But she was continually lifted out of these valleys by the comfort of familiar, loving faces, there to ease their minds with one glance at the Christina they knew and needed to see: friends from her church, the wives of the church elders, family members and friends from Port Angeles.

Christina tried to put on a brave face whenever she was aware of someone there to see her. But there were times that she didn't even open her eyes when someone came in the room... simply too tired to talk.

In one moment of wakefulness, she sat sipping her water, her father sitting on a chair at her side. Her mother stood in the doorway chatting with Paddy, her nurse from the night before. They seemed to have reached an impasse in their conversation, with Paddy looking intently in Christina's direction.

Christina smiled at Paddy's quizzical look, slurping the water through the straw, enjoying the bubbly noise that sounded like childhood.

As Paddy continued to study Christina, JoDee asked, "Hey Christina. How did your surgery go?"

Christina gave her mother a confused look. Paddy was studying her, waiting to see if this girl who sat making funny sounds with her straw was someone who really knew the results of her surgery.

Then, Christina understood what her mother was asking her to do. "The surgery went well. They got most of the tumor out and it's cancerous."

Paddy shook her head, a disbelieving spirit admiring the Lord's peace at work in Christina.

Christina went back to slurping her ice water, her father looking on approvingly.

· · · · · · · · ·

That afternoon, Christina woke, the pain in her head pulling her from a restless sleep. She moaned. JoDee's worried face immediately appeared.

"Christina?" she whispered.

"My head..." Christina mumbled. "It feels like I'm lying on a wooden board."

JoDee's eyes flickered with confusion. She glanced at the cushy pillow underneath Christina's head.

"Nooo..." JoDee said gently. "You have a nice soft pillow under your head."

"Huh," Christina said, disappointed that the pain couldn't be remedied by a quick removal of the board. She fell back to sleep.

· · · · · · · · ·

The next morning Christina woke to a sleeping Linsey on the chair next to her bed. She stared fondly at her best friend, overwhelmed with affection for her and humility at Linsey's sacrifice over the past two weeks. LOTS of people had been in and out of the home Linsey owned on Pettygrove Lane. All life had pretty much stopped to accommodate appointments, visits and surgeries. Everything had been revolving around Christina. And Linsey had been right at the helm, keeping that wheel of support and encouragement efficiently spinning.

And here she lay... or rather, curled.

As if sensing a watcher, Linsey's eyes opened. She smiled sleepily at Christina.

"How you feeling?" Christina asked.

"Ugh. Stiff." Linsey stood up and reached her arms to the ceiling. "How are you feeling?"

"Good!" Christina said. "My eyes are still pretty funky. I keep seeing weird things with them. Like, you look a little funny to me right now."

"Well, I'm not sure if that's your eyes or if I'm indeed just funny-looking right now," Linsey said with a tired smile.

Before long, Doug and JoDee walked in.

"How's your cold?" Christina asked her mom.

"A lot better than your head, I'm sure," JoDee chuckled.

"How you feeling today Christina?" Doug asked.

"I still feel good."

Just then a doctor walked in. He looked familiar to Christina.

"Hello," he greeted. "I'm Dr. Branson. I was in your surgery yesterday."

Christina nodded. "I remember you."

He talked slowly, his hands moving with his flowing words.

"I just wanted to tell you about the surgery that I witnessed yesterday. I've seen Dr. Crowley work a few times. But I've never seen him work like this before."

The family was all ears.

"Once he realized from the angiogram that it wasn't a meningioma and would not be easy to get out, Dr. Crowley planned on just removing a small section of the tumor for a biopsy. So, he did that... and then he stood there for a while studying the computer screen." Dr. Branson paused in his speech, as if mimicking Dr. Crowley standing before the screen. "Then he decided to remove one more small piece that seemed safe to get at. Then, he stood there looking at the screen for awhile more," Dr. Branson paused again, "and then decided to remove another piece." He stopped, his hands carrying on a visual demonstration of tumor removal, cupping and scooping. "And all the while that he was removing pieces of the tumor, your brain was filling in the spaces he was opening up." His hands pressed into each other. His face was a sheet of awe. "He did

101

this until the tumor was nearly all gone." Dr. Branson looked at each person in the room to make sure they understood the immensity of Dr. Crowley's skill at accomplishing what he did that day. "He did more than he had intended to, but with all the skill necessary to leave good brain cells undamaged."

Christina nodded. "Wow."

"Praise God," Doug said.

"Thank you," JoDee said to Dr. Branson.

Dr. Branson nodded to them all. "I just thought you might like to know that. You look great by the way," he directed at Christina as he left.

They all sat in silence a moment, thanking their Lord for His divine guidance.

. . . . . . . . .

That day, Christina was still heavily under the influence of painkillers and weariness.

There were more visitors. Each one seemed to carry a reminder of her situation with their red-rimmed eyes, hoarse words and forced smiles. They were scared.

In a moment of solitude, Christina began to think... and wonder. Should I be more scared? Lord? Am I truly understanding the gravity of this situation? Christina searched for fear in her jumbled emotions. Is there despair way down there God? Am I just in denial? Am I ignoring my fears? Her thoughts drifted to Cancer, and the future. The future was dark... for its uncertainty. She could be living out her last days right now. She could be embarking on a long, slow and painful death. She could be facing a series of battles, varying in intensity and victory. Cancer was scary. It meant Death. Even if not immediate, Death was imminent. Her life and the lives of her loved ones were forever altered. Christina felt unprepared for her family's lives to be changed by her sickness. She wasn't sure she could watch them suffer at whatever she would have to go through. She could handle it, she was sure; but what would it do to her family? If only she could spare them. If only they would throw her in a room by herself when things got ugly. It was a ridiculous notion, but she longed for it just the same.

Christina sniffed and wiped her nose. *Doggone cold*! She was strongly disturbed at the scratchiness she was feeling in her throat. The thought of getting a cold at this time overwhelmed her... even more than the pains in her head.

*Okay Lord. Cancer. What do I do with cancer?*

Still scanning her emotions, she thought she caught sight of a swirling pool of darkness deep down within her spirit. She looked harder. Was she despairing after all?

*I can have cancer Lord. But I just don't want my family to have to do this Lord. Can You please just spare them?*

Christina's eyes began to fill with tears. Her nose began to pour. She wiped the liquid away angrily.

*Dumb cold!*

She tried to pray, but fear had gained a foothold and was consuming her. A whirlpool of despair was drawing nearer to her heart, and she felt its force pulling her down.

*Lord help!*

She lay with her eyes closed, letting warm tears roll down her cheeks. The beeps in the room filled her head. She focused on the beeps and tried to pray along their rhythm.

Then the beeps seemed to fade away. She had a sense of floating above her bed...above her own body even. Her eyes were closed, but her mind was full of sight. She was floating over a dark expanse, a void like that which the Spirit hovered over in the beginning. And then she saw her parents, their faces loving and centered. They were beneath her where the bed should have been, where the void was, separating the dark from the Truth. Christina looked directly underneath her body and saw her parents' arms, woven together to form a human quilt upon which she now rested. And then next to her mom and dad, she saw Dave and Tammy...and Linsey and Robbie...and Jesse and Kristin...her high school students...Nancy Stack...her pastor and his wife...Mandy...Brett...old friends from high school...old friends from college...even people she didn't know. There was a multitude. They all squeezed underneath Christina's body, arms stitched together, passing her forward into peace. Each face looked directly into her eyes, and each penetrating gaze drove out the weeds of isolation that had started to sprout in her soul. Words were being spoken. Some of them were out loud, some of them were said in the spirit, but Christina could hear them all. They were words of love, support and request about her. And as the flow of words grew in volume and passion, the arms of her supporters released her and raised up to the heavens, leaving Christina's body to be held up by their prayers.

Christina almost burst into laughter. Then she cried, tears of gratitude, not fear.

She opened her eyes. She was sitting on her bed again. The room was the same, but the murky void was gone. She had prayer-surfed away from it.

*Okay Lord. I get it. I'm not alone in this journey. Thank You Lord.*

． ． ． ． ． ． ． ． ．

That same day, during one of Christina's alert periods, Linsey came into the room excitement all over her face.

"Teena! Wesley's here!"

"Who?"

"Wesley Ohen! The guy I've been trying to set you up with!"

"What!?"

"I know!"

"What's he doing here?" Christina's head pounded a bit from her confusion and the sudden burst of adrenaline flowing through her limbs. She felt fresh pain in her skull.

"He brought pizza for us all."

"What!? How did he know to do that?"

"I told him he could," Linsey said proudly.

"Why?"

"He asked what he could do to help. I told him that we're all hungry."

"And he came here?!"

"Yeah! And he led us all through a devotional out in the waiting room!"

"He did!" Christina suddenly felt tired from all the exuberant outbursts.

"He wants to come back and see you!"

"What! Here?"

"Of course here! He's got a friend with him and they're going to come back to meet you. Your mom's going to bring them back."

"Linsey, I look gross!"

"No you don't! You're beautiful."

"Now you're just lying to me."

"Christina, you just had brain surgery. No one expects you to look like you just walked out of a salon."

"Linsey! I don't know!"

"C'mon! Teena!"

"Fine. Send him in. Let him see me in all my glory. My pee and me," Christina said pointing to the full bag of yellow liquid hanging off the foot of her bed. "Maybe he could even empty out my bag and get me a fresh one... if he's looking to help and all."

"Oh stop it! Don't worry so much. You look great! You're full of the Holy Spirit!"

"Whatever."

Linsey sat down in the chair at the side of the bed, her face a mischievous mask. "He is sooo cute Teena!"

Christina sighed. She looked down at her pale arms, peeking out from the rumpled white hospital gown. She tugged at the gown's flaps, making sure they covered her fully. "I'm not wearing a bra or anything Linsey." She arranged the wrinkles just so, to hide that fact.

"As if he's going to notice," Linsey said with a wave of her hand.

Christina ran her hand gently over her hair, sending it all swooping to the left side of her head, away from her bloody suture and brain drain.

She sighed again.

There was a gentle knock at the door. Christina looked up to see her mother standing in the opening with one very smiley faced man and another, more timid looking one. They both had their hands in their pockets and a slightly hesitant look on their faces, like they were a couple school boys meeting their sports hero.

"Come in," Christina said, knowing instantly which one was Wesley. He was tall, fair-skinned, with the coloring of one who loved the sun. His face was flecked with a day's growth of beard, and the top of his head was covered with wispy and wild hair, like a frothy wave. He not only wore the sun's glow in his attire and tan, but he seemed to bring its comforting warmth into the room.

"Hi Christina," Wesley said softly. "I'm Wesley."

"I'm Trevor," the other guy said.

"We hope we're not bothering you," Wesley said.

"No, not at all." Christina said, raising up slightly on her elbow, but trying not to disturb the masterfully placed wrinkles in her gown. "Come on in. It's nice to meet you."

Wesley stood at the foot of the bed, right next to the bag of pee. He greeted Linsey whom he knew. Trevor and Linsey shook hands.

Christina studied Wesley for a moment, startled at how handsome he was. He looked at her and they both smiled shyly.

"I really wanted to meet you," Wesley said. "I've been following your story through the emails and from Linsey. I'm so amazed at what God is doing through this. And I just want you to know that I think you are such an inspiration." One of his hands emerged from his pocket and gestured with his words. Then he returned it to the pocket.

"Wow. Thank you," Christina said, surprised by his openness. "Linsey said you brought food for my family. That was so nice of you. Thank you."

"Oh no problem at all. I just really wanted to do something to help you all, ya know."

Trevor nodded and added, "I hope we're not keeping you up or anything."

"Oh no, I've been awake. I'm sure I look like a need a nap though," Christina said flashing her hand toward her face.

"Oh..." Both Wesley and Trevor shrugged away Christina's comment. Then Wesley said, "Seriously, I feel like I'm meeting my hero!"

"Oh... no," Christina said, embarrassed.

"No really!" Wesley said earnestly.

"Well, that's nice," Christina said. Then she quickly turned the conversation on him. "So what do you do?"

"I'm a project manager for a construction company," Wesley said.

"And you work in Portland?" Christina asked.

"Mostly. Occasionally we travel."

Her mother had long since slipped out, leaving the young people to chat.

"Did I hear something about you going on a mission trip?" Christina asked, glancing at Linsey to indicate the source of her knowledge.

"That's right. We'll both be going to Burkina Faso in just a couple of weeks," Wesley got visibly excited at the topic. Both his hands came out of the pockets now.

"What will you be doing there?"

"We'll be building some houses, teaching some classes to the kids in the area." He rubbed his hands.

"Have you been before?"

"No. I've never been on a mission trip. This is my first."

"That's great. Should be really fun."

"I really think it will."

Eventually, Wesley said, "We should probably go, and let you sleep." His hands returned to the pockets. "We'll keep praying for you and what God is doing through your life right now." Trevor nodded behind him.

"Thanks a lot. I really appreciate that."

"And I'll make sure to follow along with your progress through your email updates and such."

Linsey stood up to see them to the door. "Hey, you guys should come by our house sometime...check up on the patient," she said with amazing ease.

"That would be great!" Wesley said enthusiastically.

"Yeah. Come by sometime," Christina echoed through a grin.

"I will," Wesley said. "Well, it was so nice to meet you." He was backing toward the door. Christina thought she heard Trevor say quietly, "Nice to meet you," behind Wesley.

"Nice to meet you too," Christina said with a wave of her hand.

They disappeared behind the door.

Christina took a deep breath. Linsey waited until enough time had passed, and then she squealed. "See Teena, isn't he cute!?"

Christina smiled. "Yes Linsey. He is very cute."

"You guys were soooo flirting with each other."

"What! What are you talking about? How can a brain surgery patient flirt?"

"I don't know, but you seemed to manage just fine! And he was most definitely flirting with you."

"Whatever Linsey." Christina yawned to indicate she was done with the conversation. But her thoughts were not done. *What was that Lord?*

She closed her eyes to rest, but her mind wandered to the interchange. She smiled as she realized that in his whole time in the room, Wesley had not once looked at the bag of pee.

Prediagnosis double vision basketball game with Mandy and Linsey

Christina and Linsey enjoying life just before surgery

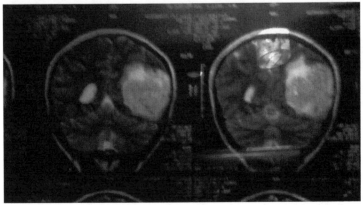

First MRI scan showing the size of the tumor (white circle is tumor tissue)

First post surgery outing with Dave and Tammy

Celebrating clean hair after surgery with brother and sister-in-law, Jesse and Kristin

Smiles and smooches from Mandy and Linsey

Christina, Doug , and JoDee

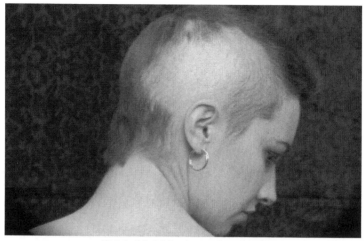

Christina's hair is beginning to grow back

Christina and JoDee--Miracle hair growing back

Enjoying God's blessings by the clear blue waters

• • • • • • • • •

Late that afternoon, the nurses came in to inform her that they needed to transfer her to a new room. To do so, she would have to move from her bed to a gurney and then they would wheel her downstairs.

JoDee, Dave and Tammy stood nervously in the room. Doug was picking up Jesse and Kristin from the airport. The wait for the transfer was long and fraught with tension. They weren't sure where they would be going and when. And the idea of moving a girl whose head had been sawed open just the day before, was quite unnerving. Christina tried to hold onto the peace the Lord had given her earlier in the day. It wasn't easy.

Finally some orderlies came into the room to say it was time to move. They asked all visitors to leave the room while they prepped all her tubes and bags for the transfer. JoDee hesitated, then left with a reassuring look at Christina.

Christina watched the orderlies. Her eyes, worse after the surgery than they had been before, were not cooperating with her. As she watched them bustle, their heads seemed to move separately from their bodies. She stared hard at them, trying to get the human pieces to move in unison. Some of her drugs had also been causing her to hallucinate, further exacerbating her vision problems. Christina felt these two issues very poignantly in this moment.

"Okay," one of the orderlies said. "You need to get on." She patted the gurney that had been sitting at Christina's bedside for over an hour.

Christina looked at them, unsure and scared. "You want me to climb onto the gurney?"

"Yes," the second orderly said impatiently. Christina looked intently at the first orderly for a sign of warmth, but at that moment, the woman's face dropped down off her head, leaving a gaping black hole set in the outline of a human skull. Christina quickly looked down at her bed, a hot tear welling up in her eye.

She sat up very carefully, feeling the pull of gravity very acutely in her head. Using her legs to slowly shift her bed sheets off her body, she gathered her gown close to her. She scooted to the edge of the bed, careful not to dislodge the catheter in her neck. The movement made her head ache. She put a hand up to the left side of her head, trying to steady the feel of fluid pain that crashed back and forth in her skull.

The orderlies watched her struggle, waiting for her to switch beds so they could move all her equipment in tandem.

Clutching her gown with one hand and her head with the other, Christina placed her feet on the cold linoleum floor and gingerly lifted her bum off the bed. The room spun. She took a step forward, raised her right knee onto the gurney and started to put her weight on it. The gurney rolled from the weight. The second orderly braced the gurney. Christina looked gratefully at her, only to gasp and quickly look away when the woman's face twisted like a pretzel.

She tried to shift her body onto the gurney, but her muscles were weak and not cooperating. She swiftly debated which hand to use as an assist. Without much thought she released her grip on her gown and used that hand to balance her body. She felt her gown fall open, baring her backside to the view of the orderlies. Another hot tear. She got her bum onto the gurney and quickly bunched up her gown around her body.

The swaying room had filled with an undulating mass of liquid darkness. The orderlies' figures swam about in the pulsing black cloud.

*Lord help!* Christina cried as the gurney began to move forward and the blackness enveloped her.

Christina closed her eyes and prayed with all her might. Her hand was still pressed hard against her head. She was seated, but the gurney was in a semi-reclined position and she was hesitant to lay all the way back onto the pillow for fear of landing on her sutures. So she leaned her back against the bed, but held her head up with her cramped neck muscles.

"Christina?"

It was her mother's voice. She opened her eyes and JoDee, Dave and Tammy, surprised at the sight of a fragile-looking Christina moving down the hall, came toward her. JoDee grabbed her arm. Tammy and Dave flanked her on either side.

Christina's eyes pleaded with her mom to help her make sense of what was happening. JoDee's face was mercifully intact, but the black liquid cloud was still surrounding everything in Christina's peripheral vision.

"Mom?" she croaked.

"I'm here." JoDee sounded strong, but her eyes were panicked.

They reached the elevator. After a moment, it opened and the

116

orderlies pushed the gurney forward. The bed rode over the door's ridges and jolted Christina's body. She pressed harder against her head and fought the cramp she could feel seizing her neck. JoDee forced her way onto the elevator but Dave and Tammy were squeezed out.

"We'll meet you down there," they shouted.

"Do you know where we're going?" JoDee hollered back, but the doors shut on her question. The orderlies stood studying the lit floor numbers.

Christina closed her eyes as the elevator descended. The motion made her stomach heave and she willed herself not to vomit.

When the doors opened an acrid smell assaulted Christina. It was the smell of infirmity. They rolled forward. Strange noises were hitting Christina in the darkness of her concentration. Yells. Moans. Squeaking wheels.

Her stomach heaved again.

"What floor is this?" she heard her mother asking.

"Trauma Care."

Christina's chin was quivering, and her eyes burned beneath her eyelids.

A scream was approaching them. Or they were approaching it. It grew louder.

"Rickeee! Rickeee!" A female was screaming this nonsensical word over and over again. "Rickee! Rickee!"

They stopped right next to the scream.

"Okay," the orderly said over the screams, "you can get on this bed now."

Christina opened her eyes. The black cloud was gone, but the room she now looked upon was dark. Dark, small, and smelly. Before her was a made bed.

Again, Christina scooted. This time, she leaned heavily on her mother as she eased over to the new bed. She kept one hand on her head and, releasing her gown, used her other to guide herself. JoDee quickly covered her with the new blankets. This bed was better positioned and Christina gingerly laid her head back onto the pillow. Her neck muscles seized up again anyway. She watched the orderlies push the gurney out of the room and heard them squeak down the hall.

"Rickeee!!!"

Christina started sobbing.

117

JoDee held her.

"Rickee!!!"

"You okay?" JoDee asked.

Christina nodded through her sobs. Then she saw a flustered Dave and Tammy appear in the door. Their faces immediately saddened at the sight of a broken Christina sitting with JoDee in a small dark room. They hurried toward the bed and lay their hands on them both in prayer.

"Rickee!!"

"*What* is that?" Dave finally whispered.

It was enough to break the tension. They all laughed.

"My new neighbor I guess," Christina said through serious sniffles.

Tammy handed her something. "Here. Put this on. Drown out the noise."

It was an IPod. With shaky hands, Christina put the ear buds in. She got as comfortable as she could, closed her eyes and, with the aid of the worship music, tried to calm down.

*Thank You Lord. Thank You Lord. You are here!*

A nurse walked in, her countenance immediately empathetic. "Christina? Hi. I'm Maxine. I'll be your nurse for the night."

Christina wiped her face, removed the buds and smiled.

"Are you in pain?" Maxine asked.

"Well..." Christina started, before sniffling again.

"They just transferred her here," JoDee stepped in. Then she looked at Christina. "It was a little hard on Christina."

"I'm sorry," Maxine said. "Let's work on getting you better situated in here." She adjusted the room's lights, creating a warmer atmosphere. Then she looked at Dave. "If you don't mind..."

"Oh, of course." Dave waved at Christina. "I'll just go call Doug and make sure he knows where to find you."

With Dave gone, Maxine checked all Christina's vitals and got her more comfortable on the bed.

"Rickee!"

"Sorry about your neighbor," she said knowingly. "She's having a spell. She'll probably calm down soon. How's your pain?"

"It's okay," Christina said, feeling much more comfortable. "I feel like I might be getting a cold though."

"Oh..." Maxine said with genuine concern.

"It's ridiculous, I know, to be worried about getting a cold when I just survived brain surgery, but..."

"Not at all!" Maxine looked at her firmly. "Colds are no fun at any time. But to be sneezing or coughing while recovering, that would be terrible. I'd be worried about getting a cold too."

Christina sniffled and smiled.

"And what do you like to eat when you have a cold?" Maxine asked gently.

Christina smiled sheepishly. "Peanut butter toast."

"I will go get you some peanut butter toast then," Maxine said. "And some tea. I'll be back shortly."

JoDee and Christina shared a glance of appreciation.

That evening, Christina basked in the warmth of her family. Her brother and sister-in-law arrived from Montana. Jesse walked up to his sister, desperate and uncomfortable. A sick sister filled him with many emotions that he couldn't quite pin down: utter sorrow, guilt, helplessness, frustration.

"Hey Christina," he said in his husky deep voice. His face was conflicted, but mostly happy to see her.

"Jessseeee," Christina drawled as she often did when she addressed her big brother. They hugged, an awkward hug around tubes and wires. "It's so good to see you."

Jesse's wife, Kristin, was a nurse and immediately put her experience to work on Christina. She removed the nodes for the heart monitor after getting permission. She gave her a sponge bath and washed her hair. Christina felt much refreshed and much loved.

Later, the Ahmanns, the Hansens, Linsey, Jesse and Kristin joined Christina in an acapella worship set. Their singing soothed the 'Rickee!' lady to quietness.

When fatigue overwhelmed her, Christina returned to the IPod and tried to sleep. Throughout that night, Jesse took care of his sister, making trips to the cafeteria when she expressed any desires for food.

The next morning, Christina woke up feeling poorly...weak and tired. Another worship service commenced, with cousin Chris playing guitar. People from church came by, singing and praying with Christina. A friend, Andrea, had even written a special song just for Christina, debuting it in the hospital room.

Later that morning, JoDee went back to rest at the hotel, discouraged by Christina's weakened state. She soon received a picture on her phone that made her heart leap with joy. Dave,

Tammy and Nancy Stack had gotten Christina out of bed, into a wheelchair, and outside. In a small garden plot in the back courtyard, with the sun shining down on her body, Christina sat in the chair with her arms raised to the heavens, singing worship songs to God. She was even smiling.

Throughout that morning, under a shower of love and prayer, Christina thought often of the vision God had given her the previous day. It was true. There was indeed a quilt of loving people holding her up. She could rest in their care.

*Thank you Lord.*

# A New Shape

*I encourage you, if you have situations in your life that just look impossible...with health, relationships, forgiveness, restored joy...you name it, God can handle it. He's just waiting for that prayer to place it back in His hands and trust Him to restore it for His glory.*

*Love,*

*Christina*

Finally!  The Lord had defeated Pharaoh, knocking him off his seat of power, bringing him to his knees in resignation.  Several hundred thousand men, women and children now traipsed out of Egypt toward the land that had been promised to them.  They formed an odd caravan: donkeys loaded down with tents, pottery, jewelry, mats and such; flocks of sheep and goats; old and young traveling on foot.

And Moses led the way.

He was feeling great.  The Lord's name was made famous in all the land and he, Moses, had been an instrument in the display.

Moses smiled as he walked.  *Thank you Lord for letting me be useful for your purposes.*  He was elated to have made it through that storm of uncertainty…facing down the Serpent of Egypt, becoming a confident messenger of the Lord, playing a part in the deliverance of the Hebrew people. Moses looked backward and scanned the human river flowing behind him. He was looking forward to some downtime with them. He wanted to get to know them, have fun with them, be a part of them. Now, with the horror behind them, he and his people could all get along.

And so, the homeless nation traveled…into the unknown… jubilant and free!

A pillar of cloud and fire led them onward until they came to the Red Sea. On its shores, the mood shifted.

Moses suddenly found himself staring down something daunting again…something familiar.

It wasn't the sight of an armor-clad army coming toward them from behind. It wasn't the sounds of the horse hooves, the trumpets, the roar of angry Egyptians. It wasn't the impassable pool of water that shimmered in their path.

What Moses recognized that set his heart aquiver, was the several hundred thousand pairs of angry eyes staring at him. He had been stared at like that before.

"Were the graves not large enough in Egypt Moses?" his people shouted at him. "Is that why you had to take us out here into the wilderness to die?"

"Yeah! What have you done to us?"

"Didn't we tell you this would happen, back in Egypt?"

"That's right! We said to you 'Leave us alone here in Egypt- we're better off as slaves in Egypt than as dead men in the wilderness.' Remember?!"

Moses looked from one face to another, his heart puddling into a soup of fear. Had Pharaoh's obstinate eyes followed him out into the wilderness? Was the Serpent of Egypt now challenging him through the stares of his own people, sucking the hope and joy from his spirit again?

*Lord! What do I do now? Why am I the bad guy again? How many times do I have to stare down a stubborn heart for Your glory?*

*Moses! Moses! Why do you cry out to Me again when trouble hits?*

The Lord's voice was unmistakable.

*Lord. Why do I make it out of Egypt, only to find that its hatred of me seems to have come along?*

*Moses. You're focusing on the wrong things. You're just seeing the problems...the disappointments.*

Moses looked out over the angry people. His heart beat faster, his palms started sweating, his skin tingled. He closed his eyes.

*Moses! I never promised it would be an easy road. There are many serpents in life. But whenever you face one, the question remains the same: Will you follow Me?*

Moses breathed deeply, remembering his promises to follow the Lord.

*Am I enough Moses? When all your people turn their backs on you, am I enough?*

*Yes Lord. You are enough.*

*Will you follow Me?*

*Yes Lord.*

*Just as I handled the serpent in Egypt, I will handle the stubbornness in my own people. Now speak to them.*

*Thank You Lord.*

Moses slowly opened his eyes, raised his arms with the staff of the Lord in his right hand and waited for silence.

"Do not be afraid," he said. "Stand firm and watch God do His work of salvation for you today. Take a good look at the Egyptians..." Moses pointed the staff at the approaching dust cloud. "...Look at them!"

Heads slowly turned around to see certain Death bearing down on them. When they turned back to him, their looks were fearful.

"Those Egyptians, you will never see them again!" Moses shouted. "God will fight the battle for you! And you?...You keep your mouths shut!"

The people looked surprised.

As Moses stared fiercely at them, their expressions began to change from fear and anger to shock and awe. The cloud that had been leading them these last several days had lifted from its position over the sea. It began to push against the winds at their back and slowly float toward them. Moses watched the white cloud glide gracefully above his own head, then over each and every head in the crowd. As it made its transit, the world went silent, like the cloud itself absorbed every single sound the world bounced upward into its folds, swallowing everything into its sufficiency. In the silence, the Lord's words could be heard by every heart.

The mass of people slowly spun on their heels to watch the

traveling cloud finally descend back to earth directly in between them and the approaching army. The sight and sounds of their former oppressors were completely removed. Now the only noise was the gentle breezes blowing over the Red Sea, lightly smacking waves of water against the muddy shores.

The faces that turned back to him were now expectant.

With the staff of the Lord in his hand, Moses turned toward the Sea...toward God's promises.

And the Lord threw the serpent into the sea.

"I will sing to the Lord,
   For He has triumphed gloriously;
Horse and rider
   He has thrown into the sea.

The Lord is my strength and my might,
   And He has become my salvation;
This is my God, and I will praise Him,
   My father's God, and I will exalt Him.
The Lord is a warrior;
   The Lord is His name."

# September 24, 2007

Three days after brain surgery, Christina left the hospital and walked into her home at Pettygrove Lane. Dave and Tammy had thoroughly scrubbed the place, leaving every surface shiny and spotless. There were flowers, balloons and candles everywhere. When she walked into her room, Christina almost cried at the sight of her wonderful bed with its cozy blankets and horde of pillows. A massive sign covered the whole wall next to her bed. The words, "Welcome home Christina" sat large on a sea of notes from her high school girls.

The cozy feel of her home matched the warm, happy feeling in Christina's heart. She felt great. She was tired yes…but she was so filled with gratitude about the relatively easy surgery and the loving support of her family and friends. She practically smiled all the time as she sat on the couch, or rested in her bed over that first day home.

Her family and friends were overjoyed at how good she looked and how nice it was to have her back home. There were concerns, of course. Christina needed sufficient rest, regular meds and space to be quiet. She was still at risk for seizures and her vision was still marred, a condition that might be permanent according to the doctor. Her eyes also continued to play tricks on her. Sometimes people's arms looked like sparklers. Her father's mouth once fell off his face when he was talking to her. Another person's smile was checkered, and JoDee's teeth once fell out.

Christina tried not to let these aberrations mar her peace. Her main concern was to continue her recovery and spend time with all the people she loved…there were so many!

The results of the biopsy were supposed to come in a few days. Until then, they just took one day at a time, enjoying each moment together.

As Christina rested on the couch that first afternoon, Linsey worked on creating a web page devoted to Christina's journey.

"Christina, so many people are following our email updates," her mother said. "I've got a list of contacts I'm keeping informed. Linsey's got a list. And people are forwarding the emails to all sorts of other people we don't even know. It would be so much easier to keep everybody informed if we just directed them to a web page."

"Okay," Christina said skeptically. It seemed weird to her to have a whole web page devoted to little ol' her. Did people really care that much to follow her story? Did people she didn't even know really want to hear about her?

Then she had to remind herself that God was providing a multitude to carry her through this, just as her vision in the hospital had made clear. And that multitude wasn't necessarily all people she knew; but it *was* all people God knew. And maybe they were following her story for a reason. Maybe God would use this to minister to someone who needed it.

"Besides, what better way to make God's name famous than tell a story about His faithfulness through brain surgery?" Linsey said from her seat in front of her laptop. "People keep commenting on how your journey is making them think about their own lives and where their priorities lay. Your story is helping people remember the important things in life."

"Well, that's great," Christina said. "People are responding to God…good."

"And your faith in Him," JoDee said with a finger point in Christina's direction.

"I suppose," Christina said, feeling uncomfortable again at the notion of praise or attention directed at her. Praise for God? Yes! Attention on God? Yes! On her? Um, no thanks. Just the thought of it sent a tingle through her buns.

Christina Ahmann's two best friends from childhood, shyness and timidity, were still companions in her adulthood. In many ways, she had lessened their hold over her. But in other ways, they still dictated a lot of her actions and feelings.

Put simply, she had severe stage fright.

· · · · · · · · ·

Christina was four years old. It was time for her first recital in her opening explorations with the violin. Her mother held recitals every year for her students: small private affairs, with family and friends of the students on hand to listen to numerous renditions of 'Lightly Row,' and the occasional attempt at Bach by an older student.

At JoDee's prompting, Christina got up to deliver her version of "Mississippi Stop, Stop." She was a little peanut with golden brown hair cut in a bowl. Matching freckled cheeks bookended a determined little face. Her stride was purposeful, the sweep of her

126

little white dress swishing around her legs like a bell-shaped flower blowing in the wind. Her arms cradled her violin, pressing it firmly against her body, as if she was afraid of dropping it. She mounted the steps of the church. She turned, not looking at the crowd of sixty people in the pews. She raised her 1/8 size violin up to her shoulder, set her soft little chin in the chin rest, raised her slender bow arm over the instrument and rested it on the A string.

JoDee lowered her head slightly, waiting for her daughter to start. Doug and Jesse sat in the back, also lowering their chins, waiting. The rest of the room had gone silent, absolutely still with anticipation.

Christina stood there, poised, ready to play, motionless.

The room waited.

Christina stood...her eyes trained on the bow...her arm resting on the string.

JoDee waited another moment. Then she stood up, and slowly approached her frozen daughter.

"Christina..." she whispered from the bottom of the steps.

Christina's eyes switched over to her mother's face.

"You can play now sweetie."

Christina looked back at the violin. She still didn't move.

JoDee mounted the steps. She moved in behind her, squatting to be at her level and grabbed her bow arm. Gently, she began to move it back and forth for Christina. After a couple bow strokes, JoDee let go, and Christina took off, pulling forth the tune from her instrument. The audience nodded along with the music, willing the girl to make it to the end.

Christina hit the last note with gusto, her bow landing firmly on the A string and holding there. Again Christina didn't move, her eyes fixed on her bow. The crowd went wild, especially affectionate over the tenderness of the scene. JoDee beamed proudly.

Christina continued to stand perfectly still, her arm a right angle in the air, her bow still pressed against the A string.

"Okay, sweetie. You can go sit down now," JoDee whispered.

The audience had since stopped clapping and now suppressed chuckles at the sight of Christina still silently poised to play.

JoDee turned and picked up her daughter by the waist, carried her down the steps and set her down in the front row pew. Christina's left arm still held the violin under her chin, her right arm still steadied the bow over the A string.

And the show went on.

• • • • • • • • •

Linsey and Tammy sat at the computer most of that day, designing a webpage devoted solely to Christina's journey through brain cancer. The address was www.christinaahmann.com.

They filled it with pictures of Christina, they wrote a short biography complete with nicknames, and they encouraged people to respond to all the updates.

Christina was impressed by Linsey and Tammy's work. She was only slightly embarrassed.

*Christina? Will you follow Me?*

*Yes Lord. Okay. If You say so, we'll put my face out there for the world to see.*

• • • • • • • • •

That first evening home from the hospital, some members of Christina's church delivered a meal to Pettygrove Lane. Christina ate with her parents, Dave and Tammy, and Linsey. Jesse and Kristin had gone home that very morning, looking slightly less anxious than they had three days ago.

During dinner, Linsey's phone rang. She got up from the table to grab it.

"Hello?...Yes! Hi!" Her face lit up.

Christina narrowed her eyes at the mischievous look on her best friend's face.

"Yeah, we're having dinner right now. The Wahley's from church brought it for us...but... we don't have any dessert."

Christina's parents were looking at her, wondering who was on the other end of Linsey's obvious scheming. Christina suspected, but didn't say.

"Sure. Brownie's would be great...Oh...well, why don't you come over here and make them?.. Great! Thanks a bunch! We'll see you soon."

Linsey placed her phone back on the counter and grinned slyly at Christina. "Wesley's bringing brownies over for dessert."

Christina felt herself blush. "Linsey!"

"Wesley..." Doug asked, "...the guy who brought us pizza...and led a devotional? He was really nice."

128

JoDee smiled knowingly.

"He wanted to know if we needed anything. And...well...we don't have any dessert, now do we?"

Christina gently cradled her head in her hands and rocked it back and forth. Then she looked up and tapped the table. "Linsey, you're not trying to set me up three days after brain surgery, are you?"

"Teena," Linsey said, her face resolute, "don't... limit... God!"

Christina shook her head.

Wesley showed up after the dinner table had been cleared and everyone was relaxing in the living room. Christina sat curled up on the couch, wearing sweatpants, a T-shirt, and a tiger patterned fleece bathrobe her mother had bought her as part of her 'recovery clothes' collection.

Wesley greeted everybody in their various states of relaxation, finally making his way to Christina.

"And how's the patient?" he asked in a jolly voice, his beaming face shining down on her. He was infectiously joyful.

"I'm good, thank you." Christina felt herself beaming as well. "Thank you for taking care of dessert for us."

"Oh...no problem." Wesley waved off her thanks. "It's the least I can do." He held a box of brownies up on display in his right palm, his left hand passing over it showily. "I hope you like brownies."

"Who doesn't like brownies?"

"Well, there's no guarantee these brownies will be like what you imagine when you say 'brownies,' because..." he leaned in and whispered, "...I've never made them before."

Christina whispered back, even though everyone in the room could hear both their whispers, "I'm sure you'll do great."

"I hope so. I imagine it's hard to mess up a 'just add water' recipe." He smiled.

"Um...I think you usually have to add eggs and oil as well." Wesley's smile dropped and he looked at the box. Christina felt bad at his dismay. "Unless you got a different kind of brownie or something."

"Oooooh," Wesley moaned. He looked up sheepishly at her over the top of the box. "Guess I already messed up huh?"

"Not at all." Christina turned slightly to shout over her shoulder. "Linsey! Can you make sure we have eggs and oil for the brownies?"

"Will do!" Linsey shouted back.

Christina smiled at him. "I won't tell anyone that you didn't know about the eggs and oil."

"I appreciate that," Wesley said with puppy dog embarrassment. "Well, wish me luck."

"Good luck."

Wesley winked and went into the kitchen. Linsey plopped down on the couch next to Christina. "I can't believe you're wearing that robe. It's ridiculous!"

"What! What's wrong with it?"

"You look silly."

"I'm comfortable," Christina said emphatically.

"But Wesley's here. Don't you want to change?"

"I am not changing for Wesley. He can see Christina as Christina, if he wants."

"Okay, silly." Linsey patted Christina's knee.

"Is he all right in there?"

"He's chatting with your mom and stirring the fluff out of the brownie batter." Linsey chuckled.

"I'm sure he'll do fine. He seems like a very capable young man."

"So," Linsey said with a sly look, "you *are* noticing him."

"Linsey," Christina said, landing on each syllable with conviction, "I'm not looking for anything like that right now. You know that."

"I know Christina. But you just don't know what God might do. Just go with the flow Christina. And don't put up your usual walls. Just let it be what it's going to be."

"We'll see, okay," Christina said, feeling weird having a conversation about a guy that she barely knew.

At that moment, Wesley stepped into the living room, a triumphant look on his face.

"Well, how did it go?" Linsey asked.

"I've made my first brownies ever! And I think it's a success."

"Careful," Christina cautioned. "Brownie success can really only be determined after they come out of the oven. It's the cooking that often destroys brownies."

"Oh." Wesley's face was mock seriousness. "Why? What can happen with the cooking?" As he talked, he walked towards the

130

couch. Linsey quickly hopped up and disappeared into the kitchen. Wesley took the empty cushion next to Christina.

"Well, so often, brownies are overdone. We call it brownie dryness."

"Sounds terrible," Wesley said.

"Yeah, it really is. But!... sometimes, in an attempt to avoid brownie dryness you can undercook them, and the middle is just a big soupy mess of brownie batter."

"And is that called brownie wetness?"

Christina chuckled. "I don't think we've actually named that mishap. But brownie wetness certainly fits."

They talked for a bit, just like two young people who've just met at a coffee shop.

The brownies came out of the oven with a slight case of brownie dryness. Realizing the only way to combat brownie dryness was to eat them fresh, everybody grabbed a spoon and cleared out the pan. Wesley chatted easily with all of Christina's supporters, including the high school girls that stopped by to check on her.

He stayed late and Christina miraculously did not get tired until he was gone. After the door shut behind him, she promptly went to bed with a smile on her face.

· · · · · · · · ·

Thursday morning, amid many tears and hugs, Dave and Tammy left to go visit their son and daughter-in-law... a trip they had delayed when they found out about Christina's emergency surgery.

They held tightly to Christina, cupping her face in their hands, telling her they loved her through quivering lips. Christina couldn't help smiling, wondering if Dave and Tammy thought the cancer might claim her life before they could get back to her after their trip, one week later.

It was emotional for Doug and JoDee as well to say goodbye to their buddies. Dave and Tammy had been such a support for the two of them through the ups and downs of the last couple weeks. Hugs were long.

With vows to return in a week, the Hansens waved out the window as they drove down Pettygrove Lane.

The Ahmanns, with Linsey at their side, stood in the driveway, hands still waving goodbye, grasping at the disappearing car.

Eventually, the metallic sheen slipped around the corner and the family was standing on the quiet suburban street, brown leaves falling to the ground around them.

They turned and trekked into a house which was a little emptier than before. More visitors were expected later that day, but already they were missing the Hansens. Doug went outside. JoDee and Christina took a nap together. Linsey set out for a business meeting.

An hour later, Christina woke up. She opened and closed her eyes heavily several times waiting to see if her vision cleared up by ferociously blinking away sleep's leftovers. She looked around the room, still seeing blurry shapes on her wall, two guitars on two stands, fuzzy curtains across her window. She sighed.

JoDee was still inert on the bed next to her. Careful so as not to disturb her, Christina breathlessly inched off the bed. Her efforts made her head hurt. She lightly touched her scalp as she walked into the living room. A tight row of staples formed a zipper along the tender incision.

Christina looked around the quiet house for her father. Peeking out the back door, she could see him hunched over a tool box. She opened the slider and walked outside into a crisp cool day, the type of day that wipes away any memory of summer with its markedly crunchy air. Her dad stood up and looked back at her.

"Hey Christina."

"Hi Dad." She sidled up to him. "You gonna fix our fence?"

"Yeah. I thought I might."

"Wow! That's awesome. It's been broken for like a year."

"Yeah, I've seen it out here whenever we've been down. I've always thought I should do something about it. And now, I've got some time," he grinned at her.

He had removed the detritus that Linsey and Christina had placed in front of the hole. Whenever they let Lucy out to relieve herself, they always double-checked the hole to make sure she could not squeeze through it, adding sticks and boulders to the pile whenever it looked suspect. Throughout the past year, an assortment of boys had come through this backyard, including a couple of boyfriends, some of them skilled carpenters. But not a one of them had managed to get to the task of repairing the damaged joint, even after several requests. And now, here was her dad, doing what he loved to do: helping out. She wondered if being able to put his hands to a task around her house helped him process and deal with the unfixable damage inflicted on his daughter's brain.

Christina threw an arm around his sweaty back. "Thanks Dad."

"Of course. Glad I can help with something around here." He smiled gently.

"I was going to go for a walk. Wanna come?"

"I'd love to. You sure you're up for it?"

"I'd like to try. I feel pretty good."

"If you get tired, we'll just come back."

They grabbed sweatshirts in the house then walked outside. Fall was making its presence known in Portland. The air felt lighter as if the cooler air had picked up all the hot sweaty grime from the summer and begun whisking it away. Orange, brown and red leaves lined the roads and formed quilts on the lawns.

"How're you feeling?" Doug asked.

"I'm good. I haven't had any hallucinations yet today."

"That's good."

"Everything's still blurry though."

"Hmmmm. Maybe a little more time will help with that."

"Yeah." Christina thought about the doctor's sobering warning that this new sight could be permanent. She studied the orange wrapped trees, willing them to clear up for her. It wasn't necessarily the end of the world to see fuzzy for the rest of her life, especially now, when Christina didn't even have a concept about how long 'the rest of her life' would be.

"It's not too bad you know, the blurry vision thing," she said, humor lifting her tone. "It's sort of like I'm looking at paintings all the time."

Doug chuckled. "You see life through Monet's eyes."

"It's pretty."

They walked in silence a bit.

"Oh, I almost forgot... Wesley called while you were sleeping."

"Oh?"

"He asked if we needed anything. I said 'no,' but invited him for dinner."

Christina said nothing, her eyes fixed on the softly outlined sidewalk. She felt confused about Wesley. Of course, it didn't take much to confuse her these days. Post-surgery, everything had become sluggish. Sometimes things moved too fast for her to follow; sometimes complex information was too much for her to handle. She felt slow on all levels.

"Was that okay?"

"Hmm?...oh...yeah. Of course. He's nice."

Doug was looking at her. She laughed nervously. "What?"

"Nothing," he said.

"Dad. Do you think his being around right now is a little weird?"

Doug shrugged. "A lot of people are interested in being here for you."

"Yeah, but I didn't know him before a couple days ago."

Doug shrugged again. "People might want to be around what God is doing here. God's glory is so evident in you. I think a lot of people are drawn to that."

Christina thought on that a moment. Part of her hoped that was all Wesley was doing here. Part of her hoped it was something else.

•   •   •   •   •   •   •   •   •

That afternoon, JoDee called Dr. Crowley's office to see if the lab results were in. Drew, Dr. Crowley's assistant, let them know that the lab at Emanuel Hospital could not decisively determine what her brain tumor was. They knew it was some sort of multi-faceted tumor, but that was it. The samples were being sent to Mayo Clinic for further analysis. It would be several days before they would hear anything more.

That was discouraging. But the encounter was heartening in another way. Drew had shared with them how many of the workers at the hospital had been positively impacted by witnessing Christina's joy. JoDee told him that many others were feeling the same way and that they had created a website where people could follow her story. Drew said he would check it out.

JoDee told Christina about that conversation.

Christina was humbled at the way God seemed to be using her.

•   •   •   •   •   •   •   •   •

That night, another round of food came to Pettygrove Lane. And so did Wesley.

More visitors were down from PA to see Christina and support JoDee and Doug. After a lovely, conversation-filled dinner, a game of Cranium began with Christina and Wesley on one team, Linsey and Robbie on the other. Christina wanted to challenge herself with games, hoping the stimulation would cut through the cloudiness and force her brain to catch up to the speed of life again.

"What's that supposed to be?" Robbie asked Linsey, pointing to the stick figure she had drawn on the white notepad.

"It's Santa Claus," Linsey said with exasperation, looking at the expired hourglass. "Come on!"

"You're the only person I know who thinks of Santa as skinny."

"What are you talking about? See his belly."

"Belly? I thought that was a basketball."

"Puh-lease."

Christina and Wesley smiled at each other as their opponents argued.

"Your turn," Robbie said with a sigh.

Wesley reached a long muscular arm across the table for the die. Christina watched him, trying not to dwell on how nice his tan arms looked. Wesley glanced up, catching Christina looking at him. He smiled. She smiled back, then looked at the board. *What is all this Lord?*

"I looked at your website today," Wesley said, his hands shaking the die. "Actually I checked it several times today." His eyes again lifted to Christina.

"Yeah?" she said.

"You have people in China putting notes on it."

"I know," Christina said.

"China, the Netherlands, Texas," Linsey added. "All over the place."

"I've been in contact with the people we'll be staying with in Burkina Faso. They've checked out the website and said they've been moved by your story."

"Wow," Christina said. "God is good."

"God is really doing something here. People are being reminded of their need for Him. He's really using your trial..." Wesley lifted a finger and leveled it at Christina, "to speak to people."

Christina was humbled by the truth of his statement. "Good. I hope people see God through this."

"I think," Wesley paused slightly, "I think some people are also seeing you through this."

Linsey threw Christina a look of wide-eyed excitement as

Wesley threw the die. Christina raised her eyebrows back at Linsey, blushing.

. . . . . . . . .

"Christina, you should write something on the web page," Linsey said the next afternoon after Christina had taken a morning walk.

"I know. I just don't know what to say."

"Just write about what you're feeling." Linsey passed a hand through the air to indicate the lack of pressure. "And talk about how God has been helping you through this." She grabbed her laptop off the desk and gently placed it on Christina's belly.

"People want to hear from you Christina," JoDee said from where she sat reading.

Christina closed her eyes, wading through the muddied world of her thoughts, trying to piece together complete sentences that she would feel comfortable sharing with the world. She sighed. "Okay. But I'll have to do this alone."

Her family watched her take the laptop into her bedroom and shut the door.

She sat down on her bed, propped the computer on her legs and stared at the screen. She closed her eyes and watched symbols float around in her mind, none of them lining up to form cohesive sentences. She sighed heavily.

*Help Lord.*

Three hours and many tears later, Christina emerged from her bedroom, her face serene but exhausted.

"There."

Her mother hugged her and Christina went to take a nap.

Linsey posted the message.

It said:

Hello Friends!

Here I sit at home, a few days after brain surgery, hardly able to comprehend what has gone on this past week. My mind still feels a bit hazy but I will do my best to sort through the fog to express some things in my heart that have been dying to get out. And then I'll have someone proofread it, so it actually makes sense:) From the bottom of my heart I just want to say thank you for EVERYTHING everyone has done. Over the past few days with visitors to the hospital (whether I was aware of it or not), the emails, flowers, and phone calls... with the ways you have all ministered to my family and friends through meals, rides, spare rooms, shoulders to cry on, LONG hours in the waiting rooms, and most of all through your passionate and unceasing prayers, I am so deeply indebted to you. At one point while I was in the hospital trying to put facts and feelings together, knowing a lot of what I was hearing wasn't "good news", I suddenly saw this very clear picture that stopped me in my tracks. I saw myself all laid out, hospital gown, tubes, IVs and all, but with no bed under me. Instead what was under me were all you wonderful people holding me up with your prayers - passing me hand over hand through the crowd as you prayed both silently and out loud. I saw distinct faces of college friends, missionary friends, childhood friends, family, even people I didn't know, and a peace just washed over me. I realized that this is not a battle I fight alone in my heart. The battle is being fought for me. I felt such a relief at that moment I almost laughed. My burden was being carried... and my job was not to "be okay" with everything and be strong for all you people, my job is to allow you all to prayerfully crowd surf me through this journey:) and to let you know why I'm okay:

I am okay because my life is not my own. I am okay because my joy does not come with the "joys" of this life. Philippians 1:21 says "for me to live is Christ, to die is gain." I am excited to live in Christ joyfully and with full abandon as long as He has me on this earth, and then for goodness sakes, I'm excited for eternity too!:) I love you all and will try to write and get back to you all as I can. My biggest prayer request today is that you would pray for my mind to clear so I can keep in close communication.

In His Hands.<br>Christina

· · · · · · · · ·

Late that evening, after everyone else had gone to bed, Christina found herself wide awake. JoDee had just finished a bath and was preparing to go to bed when she saw Christina sitting alone on the couch.

"Wesley left?"

Christina looked up from the large print Bible she was reading. "Yeah, just a few minutes ago. Linsey just went to bed."

"You guys have fun?"

"Yeah…" Christina thought back on the evening of chatting and games. "Mom?"

"Mmm-hmmm." JoDee came and sat down next to Christina.

"What do you think about him?"

"I think he's a really nice guy Christina." She paused, watching her daughter. "What do you think about him?"

"Well, obviously I think he's a nice guy."

"Anything else?"

"Well, that's what I'm not sure about. I can't tell if he's hanging around so much because he likes me or…."

JoDee put a hand over her mouth to suppress a laugh.

"What?"

"Christina, I don't think a nice, single guy hangs out with a girl and her family for four straight days unless he's interested in said girl."

"Maybe under normal circumstances I would agree. But nothing about this is normal."

"I'm pretty sure guys act the same when they like a girl under all circumstances."

Christina sighed, closing the Bible and stretching her arms over her head. "I guess that's what I'm still confused about."

JoDee thought a moment. "If this is uncomfortable for you, just tell him."

"Oh, it's anything but uncomfortable. It's so comfortable. That's partly why it's so weird. If I had met him three months ago and we were hanging out like this before all this stuff, it would have been great…it would have been perfect. But, now…I'm just not sure if it's wise to date somebody in the wake of brain surgery."

JoDee thought some more. "Talk to God. And then talk to Wesley. Make sure he understands the position you're in…find out what he's thinking about it all. Maybe just talking about it will relieve your confusion. I don't think a relationship based on love and support has to be a complication for you as you walk through cancer...in fact, it could even be very beneficial...take your mind off things you know. If that's indeed what he's offering you: love and support."

Christina blushed. "I don't even know him."

"There's time."

*Is there time?*

Gently, Christina lowered her head onto her mom's shoulder. "How's your cough?"

"Almost all gone. Just some dry coughs now and then. How are your eyes?"

"Still blurry."

"Hmmmm."

. . . . . . . . .

Tuesday night...eleven days after brain surgery; eleven days spent resting, enjoying the company of great friends. The absence of information weighed on all their minds, but it didn't run the days.

Wesley had been a visitor at Pettygrove Lane every day.

Wesley for dinner.

Wesley for dinner.

Wesley for lunch.

Christina was loving his presence. But she was also very confused. There were glances, there were conversations, there was a veritable fireworks display of sparks passing back and forth between her and him. But there had been no conversation to confirm her suspicions and answer her questions.

*What is this Lord? I didn't ask for this right now. Is this really what you have in store for me: a new relationship right after brain surgery?*

One of her worries was that a man in her life might disrupt the perfect peace she was finding with God. Sometimes earthly relationships can fill places in our hearts and minds that only belong to the Lord. Christina was feeling such a profound sense of God's presence. She didn't want a new, exciting relationship to take away from her Spirit-filled days.

But she decided to just enjoy every moment and let the pieces fall where they may.

The house was full this night: JoDee, Doug, Dave and Tammy (back from their week with their son), Linsey, Doug's family from Everett, and Wesley.

After dinner, Christina grabbed the last remaining plates from the table and carried them to the kitchen. Wesley stood at the sink, his hands gloved by soapy suds, his shirt checked with a smattering of wet spots.

"Thanks for doing the dishes Wesley," she said, laying the plates on the counter.

"Hey. No problem. I keep getting all this yummy food for free, I figure I should try to earn my keep."

"Well… all those lovely church people…I feel like I too should be earning my keep."

"I don't think so Christina. You're not supposed to be earning anything right now; just working on recovering. We're all here to serve you."

"Awww! Thanks!"

"And happy to do so," Wesley added.

"That's so nice." Christina grabbed a couple wet dishes to dry. "I think I can at least dry a couple of dishes though."

"Well, if it means you'll be hanging out with me in here, then, by all means…"

They washed and dried together in quiet. The family members moved from the dining room to the living room. They were still visible, still audible to the young people in the kitchen, but they basically disappeared from their awareness.

"So, you feeling good tonight?" Wesley asked

"I am. I'm feeling really good. I got in two good naps today."

"Lucky."

"I know. It's funny…I've always been a nap person. But I've never had such a good excuse to take so many."

"Yeah," Wesley chuckled.

"And now I have a house full of fun people," Christina added, looking into the living room at her family, then back at Wesley.

Wesley grinned at her, handing her a salad bowl. Christina rubbed it dry and put it away. He drained the sink and sponged down the counter.

Hanging up her towel and leaning against the counter, Christina watched Wesley spiff up the kitchen. "How was *your* day?"

"Good. Good. The framing is almost done on the house."

140

"And what comes after framing?"

"The plumbers will come in next… followed by the electrician. We'll start the siding while the subs work indoors."

"Cool."

Wesley threw the sponge into the sink, leaned against the counter himself, and stared at Christina. She stared back, thinking that this was their first uninterrupted eye contact since their first meeting.

He had such pretty blue eyes. Their color wavered like an image through the steam of a baking hot road. Or maybe it was her blurry vision that made his eyes waver. Christina smiled, pleased about his eyes nonetheless.

Realizing he was still looking at her, Christina tried not to blush. He smiled and then looked down at the floor. Then he glanced over at the chatting group in the living room and, with a hinting glance at her, slid down the cabinets to the linoleum floor.

Christina let her legs slowly fold, lowering her to the floor also, feeling the wood on the cabinet gently rub against her back. The floor chilled her bum, but quickly warmed to her presence.

Wesley smiled, as if they now shared a secret on the kitchen floor that the rest of the family was no longer privy to. Christina smiled back.

"Lots of new responses on the web page today. I think more people are reading it now that you've started writing on it."

"Yeah, well, I don't know about that." Christina shifted slightly to accommodate her long legs, curling them up underneath in a yoga pose. As it always did, the mention of the web page cleared out Christina's hazy brain, like spiritual sunshine breaking through worldly fog. "It's all very cool though. Did you hear Linsey put a counter on it, to see how many visitors it was getting?"

"Yeah. She told me. Pretty impressive."

"Well, it's all God. They're not there to see me."

"Welllll…" Wesley said, "they're a little bit there for you. I know I am. You're awfully appealing, you know."

Christina blushed again. "No, really. I mean, that's nice and all, but whatever people may find appealing in me comes from God. So, they're really there for Him, you know."

"I know what you mean."

"Apparently, some people have been using our updates as morning devotionals. Had no idea 'bout that."

141

"That's really cool."

"It is. It makes you think extra hard before you write an update though. Don't want to just flippantly write about this whole thing. I want to speak Truth about God always… bring Him glory….but, of course, remain true to myself and the situation."

"Well, if you're doing that: remaining true to yourself and the situation, then God will be glorified, right? He's always glorified in Truth."

"That is true," Christina said, impressed by Wesley's depth. "Thank you, for that."

Wesley nodded. They both shifted positions, responding to poking complaints in their sleepy feet. The floor was cold again underneath Christina's bum from moving to a fresh patch of linoleum. She liked the coolness of the floor, for the company was making her quite warm.

"You know," Wesley said quietly, leaning in as with a secret, "I think this is the first time we've had a chance to talk alone."

"I think you're right," Christina whispered. "I kinda like it."

"I do too."

They both looked down at the floor, suddenly shy.

"You know, I'd really like to have you over to my house sometime. Get out, show you my world."

"I would love to see your house."

"Cool." Wesley paused. When he spoke next, his voice took on a goofy tone. "Well, I could, you know, like, ask you out on a date, or something, if you'd like to go…you know, if you want to."

Christina laughed at his mock awkwardness. Then she grew serious.

"You *do* know that I just had brain surgery…right?"

Wesley's face turned earnest. "Oh well, if this is not a good time, we could just wait until you're feeling better…if you don't have time now or something."

"Oh… I've got time. Time is not the issue." Christina looked skeptically at him, urging him to make sure he considered 'the issue.'

"Well, in that case…how about this Friday night?"

Christina paused before answering, a questioning smile still on her face. Then, in all sincerity: "I would love to go out with you this Friday."

"Great!" Wesley said, a hint of relief in his voice.

"Does that mean I won't see you again until Friday?"

"Oh," Wesley was stern, "I'll be here before then...if you still want me around."

"I want you around," Christina said softly.

"Then I'm here."

•  •  •  •  •  •  •  •  •

The next day the wait ended. Dr. Crowley called.

She listened. She asked a couple questions. She hung up. She prayed.

Then she walked out to where her mother was reading in the living room.

"Doctor called."

JoDee looked up.

"The lab report's in."

JoDee braced.

"I have a mixed glial tumor...high grade...grade 3 or 4... He called it part fast-growing 'astro,' and part slower-growing 'oligo.'"

JoDee's head nodded imperceptibly, her mind placing this information within the limited amount of knowledge that she had. High grade, she knew, was bad...especially if it was grade 4...that's really bad.

"I guess it's pretty rare," Christina continued.

Christina could feel that her mouth was almost turned up in a smile and she really couldn't understand or explain why. Maybe it was her getting used to the fact that every time they heard something new, it was bad news. Regardless, the name of her tumor, and it was a pretty heavy name, could not nudge out the peace of God that she had been experiencing so strongly for several months now. Maybe a smile was her personal reminder of that truth.

Her mother's mouth was not curving upward. It was a straight line... maybe quivering?

Christina immediately felt saddened as she recognized the weight her words had just planted on her mom. Sometimes she forgot that other people had been sitting around waiting for the last twelve days also. Their lives were just as intensely impacted by the news she had just received.

JoDee said, "I'm going to go for a walk."

Christina watched her mother walk out the door, wanting to brush up against her as she walked by to take some of her sadness away.

143

JoDee walked out the door a lonely soul. When she returned thirty minutes later, she was accompanied by the Spirit of the Lord.

The line of her lips was still straight, but now with resolution. JoDee immediately sat down at the computer, freed to research brain tumors.

Here's what she discovered:

Where brain tumors are concerned, there is a lot in the name. Brain tumors aren't tidily named after the first person to discover them. ("At first I thought I had a Jones, but, apparently I have it worse: it's a Smith.")

Tumors are named based upon the World Health Organization classification system. There are several elements to each tumor name. One element is its location in the brain. A tumor found in the medulla is called a medulloblastoma. A tumor in the meninges of the brain is called a meningioma.

Another element of a tumor's name is the type of material that gave rise to it in the first place. A tumor made of glial cells, the supportive tissues in the brain, is called a glioma. An ependymoma comes from the ependymal cells. Christina's tumor stemmed from two types of glial cells: astrocytes, cells that store information and nutrients for the brain's nerve cells; and oligodendrocytes, cells that form a covering layer for the brain's nerve fibers.

After tumors are named, they are assigned a grade, a categorizing of their appearance and behavior relative to normal brain tissue. In order to accurately grade a tumor, a pathologist has to examine a sample of it. He/she determines how "normal" the cells that comprise the tumor look. This 'funny-looking' quality, along with the tumor's perceived growth rate and infiltration activity, combine to give the tumor a grade from I, (least aggressive,) to IV (most aggressive.)

If we named people in a manner similar to brain tumors we would have to finish this story calling our protagonist, "happylovingChristianPortlandigirl, very cute." But as anyone can tell you, a list of describing words can never adequately make a person known. Names and description, no matter how precise and pictorial, are simply not enough.

Unfortunately, the same can be said of brain tumors. Even though scientists and doctors have tried very hard to provide understanding with this classification system, it is quite clear that there is a lot more to a tumor than its name. Every brain tumor is different.

After several hours, JoDee closed her laptop, feeling spent. There was only one known conclusion from all her research: something serious was threatening the life of "happylovingChristianPortlandigirl, very cute."

That night, Christina sat on the couch with her parents. They prayed fervently. They praised God that His peace was still present. They prayed that the Lord would continue to open the right doors for them as they moved forward into treatment.

In a moment of silence, Christina took the mantle:

"Lord, thank You so much for how You've been here for us these last three weeks. Your peace has been sooo real, sooo comforting. You've brought all these amazing people around to experience it too. Thank You for that God. Let all the people involved in this truly know You and Your love for them. As we move forward God, we really just want Your name to be glorified in all that we do. We trust You Lord, to take us through the next steps. And You are enough for us Lord. If nothing else can be done for me Lord, You are enough. If there are many days left for me Lord, You are enough." Christina paused feeling her emotions crawl up her throat. "Be enough for those around me Lord." She sniffed heavily, feeling her parents' hands squeeze her knees. "Lord, just make Yourself famous through us."

Once they finished their communion, the family discussed the location of their next move. They talked through all the research JoDee had done on Mayo Clinic, Duke University, MD Anderson, and the University of Washington.

"It's up to you Christina," JoDee said.

"We can go anywhere," Doug echoed. "Don't worry about time, distance, finances…we'll make it work…no matter…"

Christina, not normally a decisive person, said unequivocally, "I want Seattle. I want to be close to home."

Her parents waited a moment to see if there was anything else. There wasn't.

"Okay," said Doug, "Seattle it is."

JoDee got up. "I'll go call them right now."

• • • • • • • •

Wesley and Christina went on their first date that Friday. With everyone else gone for the week, JoDee was left for the first time since the surgery to be alone with her thoughts in the Pettygrove house. She was a bit apprehensive about being alone; Christina was *really* apprehensive about her mother being alone. But JoDee passed the time with worship music in the CD player and prayers in her heart. She specifically prayed for her daughter as she watched the young couple walk out the door. It made her nervous to see her daughter's heart being pursued at this fragile time...she prayed for Truth and Faithfulness to prevail in the relationship.

That night, Wesley took Christina to dinner and then, as he had requested, they went to his house.

In his rec room, he popped in a video with footage of the youth group of which he was a leader.

They sat, semi-reclining on a large L-shaped couch, Christina on one segment, Wesley on the other, their heads meeting in its elbow.

Christina reached an arm up over her head, stretching out her side muscles.

She felt a brush of calloused skin on her hand. She looked up to see Wesley's hand greeting hers.

"What's this?" he said, looking up at her.

"My hand," she drawled.

"Oh," Wesley said. He closed his fingers around hers. "I'm gonna hold it."

"Okay..." she said with a smile.

•　•　•　•　•　•　•　•　•

The next morning, Wesley picked up Christina at Pettygrove Lane and drove them out to the little town of Cannon Beach on the Oregon Coast. The place held a special place in Christina's heart, for she had spent her last summer as a college student out there working at a small Christian camp called Canon Beach Conference Center. It held many good memories of a life lived under fewer clouds of concern.

It was a rainy day. The gray wind pressed against the town with an unrelenting wetness.

The two didn't mind. They walked the beach anyway, huddled under rain jackets, hands clasped together, shoulders bumping into each other over and over again.

Conversation was easy and light through coffee, lunch and wanderings.

146

After getting soaked and drying out in a restaurant, they headed back to Portland.

Christina sat in the toasty car, her feet warming up for the first time all day. She sat comfortably in the silence, thinking about things that needed to be said.

Finally she asked, "So, Wesley, does it scare you that I have brain cancer?"

Wesley shrugged his shoulders, lifting and dropping them quickly, like a hiccup. "No, it really doesn't."

"Why not?"

Wesley's shoulders hiccupped again. "Every day is a gift Christina. For all of us. I consider it a gift to be here with you on this day. I try not to worry about what tomorrow brings."

"You *do* know that I might die from this, don't you?"

"Ten out of ten people die Christina," he said, glancing at her. "Why is this any different? Is God different because you have brain cancer? Is God less God because you might die from it?" He shook his head, eyes on the road.

"Yeah, but...I could go bald...with whatever treatments come up."

"You don't fall in love with someone's hair."

Christina looked past the use of the word 'love' and pressed again. "Yeah, but, it's something to consider."

"You go bald, I go bald," he said, flashing her a brilliant smile.

Now Christina's shoulders hiccupped. She shook her head and looked out the window. Lord, who is this guy? Is he for real?

"But," she pressed, "does it seem like a good idea to you to start a relationship with a girl who just found out she has brain cancer."

"Christina," he said, "I'm just trying to serve God every day. He didn't give us a spirit of fear, now did He? So, I see a pretty girl that He's brought into my life, and I'm trying to serve Him as I start hanging out with that pretty girl. I'm not afraid." She watched him as he talked at the road, his fingers gesturing enthusiastically from their position on the steering wheel. Then he looked over at her and gave her another winning smile, a genuine smile. "Look," he said, "I'm not afraid of this. If you're willing, then I'm willing."

She looked forward. Was she willing? Was she willing to put him through whatever lay down the road? Was she willing to let him walk that treacherous path with her? Was she willing to jump into two unknowns simultaneously: a future with cancer and a future with

147

Wesley? Her feet were beginning to get uncomfortably hot. She turned the air down.

"After I met you in the hospital, I just could not get you off my mind." Wesley's eyes were staring intensely at the road. "I was thinking about you all day, every day of the week and twice on Sundays. So, I said to God, I said: God, if this isn't what you have for me, then you better get this girl off my mind! Seriously God!"

Christina's eyes opened wide.

"And He didn't remove you from my thoughts. In fact, I felt Him pushing me towards you."

"Have you ever felt that before?"

"No! Absolutely not! And I'll be honest with you: I've had a lot of relationships. But they've never, ever felt like this before. I mean, I feel like God is at the center of what we've got going on here. Like He's the glue holding us together."

"I feel that too." Christina let a breath out quietly. It was heavy talk. Christina had been feeling that she needed to let her walls down with this man; let him in; to believe his words; to let the irrational be possible. Life was short...why hold back?

"What's your past experience with relationships?" Wesley asked.

"Well..." Christina made a snap decision to just dive in...to trust this man, something that normally took months for her to do. "Well, in the past, I've tended to enter relationships with my guard up. I haven't wanted to let people in too quickly, just in case, you know."

Wesley nodded.

"And I've always over-analyzed things: is this going okay? Is he doing all he should if he is serious about this? Am I giving away too much of my heart? Is this going to end down the road? Should it just end now?...you know...that kind of stuff. All that questioning and analyzing and guarding...I would say it probably made it difficult for guys I've dated in the past." Christina chuckled. "And it was tough for me to truly enjoy time with them because it was all so serious to me."

Wesley glanced at her, listening in his look.

She took a breath. "I don't want to do that...now...with this."

He glanced over again, happy.

"I want to just step wholeheartedly into relationship, believe and trust...give of my heart, and let somebody...let you in."

Wesley was grinning now.

"Who knows, I might not have much time left anyway. Why wait?"

She watched the trees slide past them outside her window. She contemplated her last statement. That's right. Why wait? Why not trust this man, and let it be a glorious gift from God? Enjoy it Christina. Enjoy every precious moment you have.

She looked over at her grinning companion. "What about you?"

Wesley sobered. "Well… my experience would probably be the exact opposite of yours. I tend to jump feet first into relationships, give my heart all the way…and then, they just sort of fade, and then they're done."

Christina listened, wondering if his words should be seen as repentance or a warning.

"But I don't want to do that anymore. I've told God that I'm done with that."

She decided to go with the repentance theory.

"In fact…" Wesley paused a moment. "…this summer, I had a brief relationship…"

Christina thought back on the 19-year-old who took her spot at bowling.

"…it was really brief. And I was just so disgusted with the whole thing that I told God that I was done dating. I said to Him, 'God, the next relationship I have will be my last one.'"

That was quite a statement. Christina raised an eyebrow when he looked at her.

He studied her a moment, willing her to understand.

*Okay Lord.* And she believed.

•  •  •  •  •  •  •  •

The next week and a half, while Christina floated freely overhead in the warm currents of love, her family toiled under the gravitational pull of reality as they got everything ready for a move to Seattle. Whatever the treatment would be, they knew they just needed to be ready to uproot and plant north in an instant.

The family did not have an oncologist yet to direct them from one step to the next. Since Christina's procedure had been an emergency surgery, they had been flying solo from the beginning. JoDee had to wade through the unfamiliar systems of medicine, pathology, mail, appointments, and hospitals. Almost every day she prayed: "Lord please make me smarter than I am." There were clear moments when she felt the Lord nudging her in the right direction, with a question here, a name there, an appointment graciously given to them out of order.

All these actions and reactions took place under the sense of time lapsing. Each day that went by felt like one wasted chance at starting treatment. And while no one in the medical establishment would say to them that there was a definite urgency to their moving forward, the assignation of a grade III to her tumor was enough of an incentive for the family to press forward as quickly as they could.

Finally, by the grace of God, an appointment was set up with Dr. Thompson at the UW Medical Center for Oct 15th.

Unfortunately, a misunderstanding led to all of Christina's slides and reports traveling the pace of a snail through the post. JoDee took it upon herself to track down every document again and bring them by hand to the tumor board at the UW.

October 13th, Saturday night at Pettygrove Lane, Christina and Wesley spent the evening hanging out, desperately grasping at their last moments together before they went separate ways for two whole weeks. The next morning, Christina would be driving to Seattle for an indeterminate amount of time and Wesley would be on a plane for another continent.

They sat in comfort on the couch, legs intertwined. The house was dark except for a lamp next to them. JoDee and Linsey had already gone to bed.

The two continued the conversations they had been having for the last two weeks. The whirlwind of their relationship meant that their talks were still filled with 'get-to-know-ya' questions.

"Okay, another posting on 'WesleyOhen.com,'" Christina said, popping a piece of popcorn into her mouth.

"Okay, I'm ready." Wesley was massaging her right foot, his strong hands pressing and squeezing.

"If you could meet any one person, who would it be?"

Wesley looked up to the ceiling, pursing his lips. "Dead or alive?"

"Sure…dead or alive."

"In that case, I'd have to say Jesus."

Christina laughed.

"I mean, isn't there only one answer for that? Shouldn't we all want to meet Jesus if we could?"

"Yeah, I suppose there is only one answer. Although, technically, we already *have* met Jesus."

"This is true. But I think it would be pretty awesome to meet the actual man, have a conversation with him, spend the day with him, maybe build something with him."

"Yeah. You guys could bond over construction."

"Yeah." Wesley was staring at the ceiling again, picturing the meeting. A small smile turned his lips.

He looked back at her, his eyes bright. "How about you?"

"Oh come on! Like I could give a different answer. I'd want to meet Jesus too. You basically answered it for both of us."

Wesley grabbed her left foot, studying it a moment before working into her muscles.

She watched him work. "You're good."

"Not as good as you."

She shook her head.

"No, really. I've been the recipient of your massages. I am *not* as good as you."

"I do have a little experience."

"And it shows."

She smiled.

"You excited about going to Seattle tomorrow?"

"Yeah, I'm pumped about going to Seattle for cancer treatment! Yeah, baldness!"

Wesley smiled.

"I *am* looking forward to moving ahead in this process instead of just sitting around doing nothin'. You are going to visit us, right?"

"Christina, I fully plan on going up there every chance I get...once I get back from Africa of course."

"What? You don't want to commute from Africa to Seattle for a weekend?"

Wesley squeezed her foot. Then he glanced at his watch. It was midnight.

"You should probably go, huh?" Christina said.

"I don't want to," he said, his look soft.

"You have an early flight."

"I can sleep on the plane."

Christina crossed her arms. "You should go. You don't want to be exhausted when you get there. You have important stuff to do."

151

Wesley sighed. "All right." He squeezed her foot one last time before she lifted them off his lap. They stood up together.

He grabbed her hand as they walked to the front door. They turned to look at each other. The refrigerator was humming in the kitchen. Christina could see in his eyes that he wanted to kiss her. Her nerves immediately went into high gear and she felt her hands get clammy. She wanted him to kiss her, but these moments were always proceeded by a brief moment of dread that it would not go well.

She noticed that, from this distance, Wesley's face was perfectly clear. There wasn't a blurry line anywhere on his beautiful face.

"I can see you perfectly."

He smiled. "I'm glad."

Wesley leaned down, his breath warm against Christina's cheek.

It was a sweet, long kiss. Christina felt her arms riding up his shoulders and connecting behind his neck. She could feel his doing the same behind her back.

After a few moments, they pulled back and looked at each other with smitten eyes.

Wesley blinked heavily. "I think I need ta sid'down," he said with a big breath.

Christina laughed. Wesley leaned backward against the wall, pretending to be dizzy.

They said farewell. Christina watched his car disappear into the dark night.

*I don't know God...but... thank You!*

• • • • • • • • •

Sunday, Christina and JoDee packed the car and drove to Seattle. Doug would meet them there from the other direction.

As they drove I-5 North, Christina sat in the passenger's seat, watching the Columbia River pass underneath them. She could see ripples on the water's surface.

"Mom, my eyes are totally getting better."

"That is so great Christina."

A few days prior, they had been overwhelmingly and surprisingly blessed. A lovely family, friends of Linsey's parents in Sequim, WA, had offered the use of a house in Seattle for as long as they needed it. This family had battled the father's cancer in that very house the year before. And now they wanted Christina to do the same.

That Sunday, the Ahmanns and Linsey's family walked into the house and almost cried. It was beautiful. Cute and charming on the outside; newly remodeled and modernized on the inside. It had a gas fireplace, a Jacuzzi tub, three bedrooms, a beautiful kitchen. It was fully furnished and brimming with food that JoDee's sisters had purchased for them. It was ten minutes from the UW Medical Center. It was perfect.

They dubbed the abode 'The House of Strength and Courage,' after Joshua 8:1.

Christina settled in, ready for whatever came next. The Lord had been with them every step of the way. Now, He had made a place for them here, quite literally. She just needed to walk forward in faith.

· · · · · · · · ·

The University of Washington Medical Center is a good hospital. Its alliances with the Fred Hutchinson Cancer Research Center and the Seattle Cancer Care Alliance enable it to provide the most advanced treatment for cancer patients possible.

Christina had chosen the UW less for its record than for its proximity to her life in Portland, her roots in Port Angeles and her budding relationship with Wesley. Doug and JoDee were perfectly pleased with her choice, for the above reasons, and because it was a great place to receive treatment for an anaplastic oligoastrocytoma.

Their assigned oncologist would be Dr. Marc Thompson. They had spent the last few weeks of this adventure traveling the roads of medicine without a Fyodor's 'Book of Cancer' to assist them; just the Internet and the jigsaw pieces of information they had received at each step.

"I'm going to be your quarterback," Dr. Thompson said upon meeting them.

Doug, JoDee and Christina all sighed. "Thank you," Christina voiced for them all. "We really appreciate that."

"Yes, we've been pretty alone up until now," JoDee expressed.

"I know. That happens when you have to have an emergency surgery. Sounds like things have gone well though. I've seen your report, and --- "

"What?" JoDee said. "You've seen the report?"

"Oh, yes. The board has reviewed it."

"It came in the mail before we got here?"

"Yes," Dr. Thompson nodded with gentle confusion.

"They told us it wouldn't get here on time. So I hustled to get another copy to bring with us," JoDee said, holding up the stack of paperwork she held on her lap.

Dr. Thompson smiled a sympathetic smile. "I'm sorry you had to do that. The report made it on time."

JoDee glanced at Doug who put an arm around his wife. She shrugged her shoulders and chuckled.

"Like I said," Dr. Thompson said, "I'll be your quarterback from now on. Hopefully, we can avoid any more stress and misunderstandings."

"That sounds great!" Christina said boisterously.

Dr. Thompson had that way about him; comforting. He was gentle yet reassuringly firm. His white hair glowed with wisdom, and his soft face crinkled with compassion. "So, as I was saying, I saw the report and it looks like you had a really great surgery."

The Ahmanns nodded.

"I mean really great."

"We thought so," Doug said.

"You have an anaplastic oligoastrocytoma," Dr. Thompson said, studying his own set of records on the computer screen. "Fairly rare."

"We've heard," Christina said. "So, what's your prognosis?" She wanted to get it out there and done with. The family had each been dealing with the possible limits to Christina's life for several weeks now. It was time to let an expert weigh in.

Dr. Thompson studied her for a moment, searching her eyes for hints of maturity or understanding, or something to indicate what type of response she would have to his answer. "Are you sure you want to know?"

Christina nodded, slowly, assuredly.

"Whyyyy don't you tell me what you know, first," Dr. Thompson said, drawing out the 'why,' as if stalling.

Christina smiled, recognizing his skepticism. "I have a high grade cancerous tumor. It's life threatening. I might not have much longer." She threw in a slight grin at the end of her words.

Dr. Thompson furrowed his brow, then glanced at her parents

to read their reactions as well.

"Okay. Well, average life expectancy for your type of tumor is… about 4-7 years."

He paused, letting the number sink in. The nebulous form of Death was starting to take a little more shape, be a little more visible.

They all nodded. It was actually a significantly larger number than the ones they had been prepping themselves to hear. For all they had known up to that moment, Christina's tumor was growing again, attacking her vital pieces, using up her minutes. They had come prepared for the statement, "You should be saying your goodbyes." So to hear the word 'years,' the Ahmanns were, in all actuality, relieved. JoDee's heart was doing back flips. She had asked God for five more years with her daughter. Maybe she would get them.

In the immediate wake of her relief though, Christina was contemplative. Four to seven years. To hear a very specific limit placed on her life was bizarre, difficult. She would have to think about this for a while.

Dr. Thompson, getting no strong reaction to his prognosis, decided to move on to discussing treatment.

"As far as treatment goes, I'll just tell you up front that my recommendation will be different from my colleagues. In fact they would not agree with what I'm going to tell you. But, I've just written a study on treatment options for brain tumors such as yours that argues against the use of chemotherapy and radiation simultaneously. Most oncologists would prescribe them both to you at this point. But, I'm a statistics guy and right now, research is showing that just radiation first is the best treatment. Chemo can come later, if necessary."

He went through a litany of statistics from his as-yet-unpublished paper arguing his point. The Ahmanns sat in rapt attention.

"If this sounds contrary to what you had in mind, then I can send you to one of my colleagues and they will get you on a program. If you decide to stay with me, we'll begin radiation right away."

He paused, letting them think.

They didn't need long.

"Sounds good to me," Christina said, glancing at her parents, who nodded. "Let's do radiation."

"Okay. Radiation it is." Dr. Thompson typed something onto the computer.

"When do we start?"

"Well. I can set up an appointment with Dr. Ramsey for tomorrow. Or…" he glanced at the clock on the wall, "…if you're not doing anything, you can just go over there now. He's in, and I'll tell him you're coming. He could get the ball rolling today."

The Ahmanns looked at each other. Then simultaneously they turned back and nodded. "We'll go today."

· · · · · · · · ·

Harborview Medical Center didn't have the same tidy, academic sterility that UW Medical Center had. It's a hospital that specializes in treating trauma patients, so the pace of the facility is frenzied, with staffers hustling and bustling, gurneys and wheelchairs crowding the halls, and the sticky smell of sour sickness in the air.

The change of venues was stark to the Ahmanns as they took the elevator down into the depths of Harborview to find Dr. Ramsey, the radiation oncologist who would design Christina's radiation program. They walked in silence down a dimly lit hallway, trying not to stare at the tiles that were in the process of falling off the ceiling. Soiled sheets on abandoned gurneys threatened them with germs and smells. Wheelchairs and beds forced them to weave along the tile floor until they finally reached Dr. Ramsey's office. In this building, the reassuring meeting they had just had with Dr. Thompson receded in their minds and the shadow of Death began to darken their vision of the future.

They checked in at the receptionists' desk, where they were told Dr. Ramsey wouldn't be able to see them for about thirty minutes. They stood inert for a moment in the waiting room, aware of the stares of other patients. They decided to find the cafeteria, because Doug was hungry, a state in which he pretty much always resided.

They wove back down the hall to the cafeteria. JoDee was beginning to feel the dirty walls closing in on her. Her heart had since stopped doing back flips at God's answer to her prayers and she was beginning to feel the heaviness of Christina possibly spending her final years in environments like this one.

In the cafeteria, the smell of food replaced the smell of sickness. Doug bypassed the standard fare of saran-wrapped deli sandwiches, seeking a specialty sandwich off the grill instead.

156

JoDee stared at him. "Are you serious?"

"What? It looks good," Doug said, pointing to the picture of the BBQ beefsteak sandwich on the menu board.

"You can't be that hungry Doug. We just ate an hour ago." JoDee had in her hand a tray with a small cup a soup. Christina carefully set an apple on her mother's tray, looking nervously into JoDee's face.

"I *am* that hungry," Doug said adamantly.

"Doug, I don't want to miss Dr. Ramsey," JoDee said through clenched teeth.

"Mom." Christina stepped up and grabbed JoDee's tray. "Why don't you go sit down. Dad will get his sandwich. We'll pay for these things, eat, and then go back to Dr. Ramsey."

JoDee slowly released the tray to Christina's steady grip, suddenly looking like a child.

"Go sit down Mom. We'll be right there."

Doug ordered his sandwich. JoDee sat down to breathe. Christina paid for their food. Then she walked toward the table where her mother sat with her purse clutched to her stomach, her eyes on the floor.

JoDee had reached the end of her reserves and faltered. Christina sat down next to her mom and placed the cup of soup in front of her, opening the lid and letting the aroma drift up to her mother's nose. "Mom. Eat!" She handed JoDee the spoon.

"I don't like this place Christina."

"I know. I don't like it either. But Dr. Thompson said we won't be having the treatments here. We just have to come here to meet Dr. Ramsey."

"I know. Thank the Lord."

JoDee brought a spoonful of soup to her mouth and poured it down her throat. It was good.

Christina bit into her apple.

Doug showed up, a tray in his arms heaping with steam and yummy smells. He had a satisfied look on his face. "See, doesn't this look good?" he said, setting the tray where JoDee could see it. He watched her for a moment, waiting for her approval. "And it didn't take very long to make either."

He sat down, laid a napkin across his lap, picked up the first half of his sandwich and took a large bite. "MMmm," he said. "'S'good."

157

JoDee and Christina smiled at each other.

. . . . . . . . .

She would have 33 radiation treatments. The list of possible side effects was vast and varied. The most common was fatigue, ranging from a mild case of need-to-naps, to a debilitating flattening of life. Hair loss was very likely, and it would probably be permanent at the site of the treatment. Nausea and headaches were possible, and treatable. Cognitive skills could suffer, which could also be permanent. The pituitary gland could be damaged, also fixable. And, ironically, the radiation treatments could cause another brain tumor down the road.

Thirty-three times, Christina would go to the UW Medical Center, a ten minute drive from the house. She would trek to the Radiology Floor always with a family member, oftentimes with additional friends as support. The therapists would take her back into a room outlined by one-foot-thick cement walls that separated the radiation from every other living creature. She would lay down on the table, where they would place on her face a mask like something out of a horror movie. The mask snapped into the table, so that pressure was applied to Christina's mouth and nose, reminding her to remain absolutely still. The therapists would disappear behind the protective walls. After a moment of quiet, the sound of a mosquito hitting a bug zapper would fill the room for about 5 seconds. During those 5 seconds, with eyes closed, mouth pressed shut and heart beating quickly, Christina would pray.

"Lord please protect my good brain cells! Die cancer cells die!!!!! Hold on little hair follicles, don't let go!!! Lord, keep them strong!"

The buzzing would end. The therapists would return to reposition Christina. Then they would disappear again. Then the sound of another mosquito drawn to the light: BUUZZZZZZ!

"Lord make the cancer cells die!!! Diiiiiiiiiiiiiieee"

Therapists….repositioning…third buzzing.

"Go God! Go brain, stay strong yeehaw!"

Therapists…reposition…last mosquito.

"Jesus protect my brain and hair!!! Let them all come back again and heal well!! Diiiiie cancer!!!!!"

Each visit, Christina had to resist the urge to shout these prayers out loud. But, with the mask pressing against her lips like a shushing finger, she couldn't enunciate. Her prayers would most likely sound like a zombie moaning, which would only bring the therapists rushing to her side to make sure she was all right. Then they would just have to start all over again. So Christina learned to do her radiation cheers silently, content to know that God heard them.

.  .  .  .  .  .  .  .  .

The treatments were not painful. And up until halfway through the program, Christina felt no significant side affects. At one point, her radiologist called her boring...a real compliment in the oncology world. But, around mid-November, Christina began to find a daily nap, sometimes even two, absolutely essential. And her trips to the gym with JoDee grew less frequent. Her shopping forays in downtown Seattle took a backseat to quiet evenings on the couch in front of a movie and behind a bowl of popcorn. It wasn't anything traumatic...but quite apparent.

There were outside influences that aided Christina's upbeat attitude in her treatment. She had many visitors coming in and out of that house in Seattle. Plus, she was given permission to drive again, as her eyes had improved dramatically. And, of course, every single weekend that Christina spent in Seattle, Wesley came up to visit her, minus the two when he was in Africa.

Things were going well between the budding young couple. Sometimes Christina would be struck with fear about all the things that could go wrong: her death coming sooner than anticipated; Wesley getting hurt by the whole thing; her getting hurt by the whole thing. But she would just pray for the Lord to help her be soft to the possibilities, to the promises Wesley would say, to the fun they had together. Sometimes, when she was struck by the absurdity of their situation, she would challenge his commitment.

"Why are you here?"

"You are aware of what the doctors are telling me aren't you?"

"You know, you don't have to have all the right answers all the time for me. It's okay to be afraid of this whole thing...in fact, you should be a little afraid."

To each of her challenges, Wesley would assure her that he was not afraid; he was in this for the long haul; he wanted to spend every last day, every last year of her life with her.

It was too wonderful to be true. But here he was; a present and active part of her todays, and a planned presence in her tomorrows.

She learned to rely on him, depend on him, love him.

It was fun. What was radiation treatment in the midst of young love?

.　.　.　.　.　.　.　.　.

JoDee stayed with Christina in Seattle for almost the entire time. Doug would come for frequent visits on the weekends. And there were many other visitors, there to play games, laugh and just be.

There were times of course…times of uncertainty. Moments of panic, realities to face, fears to pray away.

A few weeks into her treatment, on a Thursday evening, Christina was in the bathroom examining her hair. So far those radiation cheers seemed to be doing their job, as there was no sign of hair loss.

She ran her hands slowly through her hair one more time. Her palms wrapped around the back of her neck, their coolness feeling good on her skin. Her right hand stopped at the base of her neck, her fingers finding a small lump under her skin. She palpated it. It was soft and squishy, like a liquid bubble lodged under her skin. She circled the lump with her fingers. It couldn't be bigger than a dime. But it could have been the size of a mustard seed for all Christina cared; it was new and should not be there, and that made her very nervous.

Heart pounding, she grabbed the bathroom door knob, gripping it extra tightly to get some friction on it with her clammy hands.

"Mom!"

"What?"

"There's a lump on my neck!"

JoDee set her laptop down on the coffee table and patted the couch cushion next to her. Christina hurriedly sat down, turning her back to her mother. Her fingers, which hadn't moved from their perch on the lump, now yielded to JoDee's touch. Christina kept her hand positioned on her shoulder, ready to move in again once JoDee finished her study of the lump.

"Hmmm."

"What do you think?"

"I'm sure it's nothing. You know that brain cancer doesn't spread Christina."

"I know. But what if it's something else."

JoDee smiled. "There's the girl I know."

Christina spun around to look at her. "What do you mean?"

"Christina, you've always been OVERLY concerned about every single little bump, rash, bite, or anything out of the ordinary you've found on your body. Don't you remember all the times you came to me going 'Mom, what's this?' 'It's a mosquito bite Christina.' 'But what if it's the beginning of a third arm or something?'"

Christina grinned. "Well. I do have some credibility now, what with a brain tumor and all."

"This is true. Don't you think it's a little ironic that you, who has always been afraid of things going wrong with your body, are indeed having to deal with a brain tumor?"

"Yeah," Christina smiled.

"Which is also why it was so surprising to me that you had all those symptoms for so long and never shared them with your doctor, or really shared them with any of us. That was just... so out of character."

"I know. It surprises me too when I think about it." Christina lay back against the couch, feeling suddenly grumpy about the mysterious lump.

JoDee patted her arm. "Christina, I'm sure it's nothing. But...hey...one good thing about having to get radiation every day is that you get to go to the hospital with all those great doctors. We'll ask them tomorrow about the lump. Okay?"

"'Kay." Christina lay back and watched a movie with her mom, her hand unconsciously pinching and tapping the lump throughout. She had trouble sleeping that night.

* * * * * * * * *

The next day, Dr. Ramsey was available for a brief consultation.

Christina sat sheepishly in a chair while he felt the lump. She looked at him when he finished. He was smiling at her. "I bet you're afraid your cancer has spread to your neck."

Christina said with a laugh, "Well, what if I just sprout cancer tumors all over my body."

Dr. Ramsey laughed loudly.

Christina was pleased to hear him laugh. (It was a personal goal of hers to make all her doctors laugh.)

Dr. Ramsey explained to Christina and JoDee that the lymph system ran down the back of her neck, and the lump was just refuse draining still from her surgery.

Christina breathed a grateful sigh.

• • • • • • • • •

"It's nothing," Christina said into her cell phone as she and her mom walked through the halls of the UW Medical Center. "I guess there are some lymph nodes there and they're just draining away fluid from my surgery."

On the other end, Wesley sighed in relief. "Good to know. Do you feel better?"

"I do. It's nice having all this access to doctors, ya know. Every little bump or blemish can be ruled out as any more badness."

Wesley chuckled. "Hey, speaking of potential badness, have you been following the flooding news?"

"Um, no not really." Christina and JoDee had reached the doors to the building, and through the glass, they could see more of the rain that had been pouring nonstop for the last week. "I mean, quite clearly, there's been a lot of rain. Where is it flooding?"

"Well, they're saying there's pretty bad flooding just south of Olympia, in Centralia. They say it's even reaching the height of the interstate."

"Uh oh."

"I know. They're talking about closing it down."

Christina and JoDee raced through the downpour out to JoDee's car.

"Are you going to be able to come up this weekend

"Oh, I'll be there this weekend."

"What if the road's closed? Will you drive around?"

"I'll figure it out. Don't worry, I'll be there."

"Wesley. You know you don't have to come if it's too hard."

"I want to come Christina."

"I know, but don't think that you have to. You've been here every weekend since we came. It's okay if you can't make it...you know, a flooded road seems like a pretty good reason to stay home."

"Christina, I'll be there."

Christina looked over at her mom who was listening to her half of the conversation. "All right. Keep us posted."

"I will. Call you later."

"'Kay, bye."

"Bye."

Christina hung up. JoDee was looking at her expectantly.

"Wesley says they might shut down I-5. But he says he'll be here anyway."

JoDee laughed. "He can't go a week without seeing you.

Christina chuckled, pleased.

"Want to go to the gym?"

"Umm…" Christina evaluated her energy level. "Yeah. Let's do it."

"You have the energy?"

"Yeah. I think I can do it today."

After spending an hour at the gym, half of which Christina spent lying down on a bench waiting for her mother to finish on the treadmill, the two women stood on the sidewalk in the rain. Their car was parked across the street. JoDee watched the oncoming cars, looking for an opening to cross. Slightly behind her, Christina was looking at her cell phone and walking forward. Without hesitating, Christina made to step off the sidewalk. With a quick stab of her arm, JoDee stopped her daughter from going into the road right in front of an oncoming car.

Christina looked up, shocked.

"Christina?" JoDee said in a high pitched voice. "Pay attention!"

"Whoa. Sorry." Christina was looking at the car that had sped by her. She put her phone in her pocket. "That was a close one."

"Yeah," JoDee said, her heart rate coming down again. "Too close."

They sprinted across during an opening. Inside the car, they wiped the raindrops from their eyes and looked at each other.

Christina smiled. "Can't you just see the headline?" she asked.

"'Girl steps in front of car after surviving brain surgery,'" JoDee said with a smile.

They laughed together.

JoDee started the car. "Just goes to show: any of us could die at any moment."

"Nobody knows," Christina agreed.

"Live it while you got it."

Back at home, Christina napped while JoDee worked on emails and phone calls.

Christina woke up at dinner time. Normally at this time on a Friday night, she would be preparing for Wesley's arrival. She would tidy up the house, take a shower, get Canasta cards out. But, tonight, she wasn't sure if he would be coming. She helped JoDee make a dinner, then as they ate it, they watched a chick flick. Her phone rang again.

"I have good news and bad news. Which one do you want first?"

Christina sat down on the couch, curling her feet up under her. "Oh, I guess the bad news."

"I won't be coming tonight...I-5 is closed."

Christina laid her head against the couch's arm. "Okay. I'll miss you."

"I'll miss you too. Now do you want the good news?"

"Yes."

"I'll be up at 8 in the morning... if you're willing to pick me up at the airport, that is."

"What?" Christina sat up. JoDee looked curiously at her.

"I'm on a flight from Portland to Seattle, leaving here at 7 am, arriving at 8 am. Can you pick me up?"

"Of coooourse!"

"Great! You'll have to drop me off at the airport again on Sunday at 5 pm."

"Not a problem." Christina nestled back into the couch again.

She went alone to pick Wesley up at the airport at 8 am, and the two of them spent the day shopping in Seattle together.

•   •   •   •   •   •   •   •   •

A week before Thanksgiving, Christina was in the shower, vigorously scrubbing shampoo into her hair. She stepped into the spray to rinse, her hands squishing and squeezing clumps of her hair.

Suddenly she stopped. She brought her right hand before her face, her left hand wiping moisture away from her eyes. She fearfully opened them to a soggy clump of brown hair in her hand.

"Oh."

She held the clump for a moment, as if by holding onto it, it was still hers. She felt her shoulders pinch together...curling upward in a hunching, protective way. She opened her hand and let the clump fall to the shower floor.

She ran her hand down the hair on the right side of her head again, producing another mangled clump.

"Dear Lord."

She pulled out several more clumps, the pile of hair on the floor beginning to look like a disrespectful rodent intruding upon her time in the shower.

Christina stopped pulling out the clumps, realizing there might be none left if she wasn't careful. She quickly checked the hair on the left side of her head, satisfied when a good yank yielded nothing.

She sighed deeply.

*Okay Lord. I surrender my hair. You are enough for me Lord. I give You my hair. I give You my appearance...for the rest of my life.*

Tears formed.

*I surrender Lord.*

She was repeating the words as an exercise...a reminder to herself of her need to surrender. If she said the words enough, the true surrender would follow. She would keep exercising her desire to yield.

Gingerly, Christina finished washing her hair, toweled off and dressed. Then, scowl on her face, she scooped the hair out of the shower drain, wrapped it in tissue paper and discarded it in the trash can.

She blew her hair dry, ignoring the many strands that fell out in the process, forming brown scribbles on the countertop. She carefully combed her hair once it was dry. The balding spots were actually pretty well concealed by the curtain of her remaining hair. It would have to do for now.

She came out of the bathroom, announcing her new era of radiation-pattern baldness. Her mother hugged her.

• • • • • • • • •

For Thanksgiving, Christina and JoDee traveled to Pasco to join a family gathering at her aunt and uncle's house. Doug was not going to be joining them because of a staph infection in his leg. But the house was filled with her brother (able to make the trip from Montana, albeit without his wife), her two aunts and uncles, six cousins and, a couple days later, Wesley.

The smells of feast rolled out of the kitchen into the living room where Christina sat on the couch, surrounded by her cousins. They all wanted to talk to her, touch her, experience that she was the same cousin they had always known in spite of what they had been hearing about her from their parents. Cousins Chris and Anna sat in chairs opposite her, their young adult minds grappling with what they knew Christina was dealing with. The four Van Dyke girls, Jade, Gabriela, Chloe and Laila all sat on the couch with Christina, snuggling as close as they could. Jade, the oldest at 13, was quiet, contemplative. The three youngest, 9, 7, and 5, laughed with their older cousin as they always had. Jesse lay on the floor, his head resting on his arms. Wesley sat respectfully in another chair, letting the cousins get their fill.

"So Anna, how's the theatre world treating you these days?" Christina asked, scratching over her beanie at an itch on her scalp.

"Pretty good. Actually, it was really cool…I just took a class on stage combat."

Anna flipped her newly dyed brown hair over her shoulder and sat forward in her seat with excitement.

"You mean like fake fighting?" Wesley asked, intrigued.

"That's right. It's really fun."

"Could you show us something?" Christina asked.

Anna beamed. "Sure. I need a partner."

The three youngest girls all raised their hands wildly. "Me!" "Me!" "Me-me-me-meeeee!"

Anna looked around at the sea of soft little girl arms that suddenly surrounded her. "How about we all grab a partner and do it together?"

"Yeah!" Christina cried, grabbing Jade's arm and pulling her up. Anna paired off with Jesse, Gabriela and Chloe joined hands, and Laila grabbed Wesley's arm and pulled him to her side. Chris sat and watched.

"Okay," Anna said authoritatively. "Now, for every punch or slap between two actors, there is something called a knap, which is the sound that's supposed to sound like an actual slap. Like this…" Anna clapped her hands together really hard. SLAP!!! Everybody did the same.

"Ow!" Laila whined.

"Well, don't hit yourself so hard," Wesley teased.

"But," Anna continued, "knaps do need to be really loud, because the audience needs to hear it. You can make a knap by clapping your hands, or by hitting your thigh." Anna smacked her thigh. THWAPP! Everybody did the same.

166

"Owieee!" Laila squealed, hopping around on the leg she hadn't smacked.

"Now, when you do your knap, you want to hide it as much as possible. You don't want the audience to see you making the sound. Otherwise it won't look very real, right?" Anna demonstrated a smack on her thigh that occurred mostly behind the shield of her body. Everybody tried to copy her.

"Now," Anna said, turning to Jesse, "let's say Jesse was going to slap me in the face-"

"Which I would NEVER do," Jesse interrupted, directing this line at the little girls.

"Of course, he would never hit anyone," Anna said, grinning, "but if we were actors in a show, and your character was going to hit my character, then you would swing your hand right in front of my face...close, but not too close." Anna guided Jesse's hand through the air about 2 inches from her face. "And as his hand goes by, I have to turn my head quickly, like it just got slapped, and that's when I do the knap. Understand?"

Heads nodded.

"Should we do one?"

Heads nodded again.

Jesse stepped toward Anna, swinging his hand quickly through the air at her face. Anna turned her head to the right at the exact time that she clapped her hands to the side of her body. SLAP!

"Whoa! Bravo!" Christina shouted. "Encore!"

The young girls squealed with delight. "It looked so real!" "Do it again!" "Can I try?"

Anna and Jesse bowed, and then Anna said, "Why don't you all try it now?"

Christina turned to Jade and said, "Wanna hit me, or want me to hit you?"

Jade grinned. "I'll hit you first."

"Okay...just don't hit my beanie off," Christina said jokingly. "Wouldn't want to scare y'all."

Jade pulled her arm back and swung it towards Christina. Christina threw her head to the left. She was concentrating so hard on turning her head at the right time that she forget to do the knap. She looked back at Jade, then clapped her hands loudly. SLAP!

Jade dissolved in laughter. "A little late there Christina."

Christina shrugged. "It's the tumor. Throws my timing off."

167

Jade's face flickered for a moment as if she wasn't sure if Christina was kidding. Christina grabbed her in a quick one-armed hug. "My turn to smack you."

They played that way for a long time. They tried punches, wrestling moves and knock-downs. The girls amped up on the physical fun. Christina never did get the timing right.

Finally they settled down and Anna brought out a massive case of theatre makeup and turned the girls into trees.

Sunday morning, the group planned to go to the Newbury's church in Pasco. Cousin Chris, who would be leading worship in the service, with Jesse playing along on his cello, asked Christina on Saturday if she would be willing to get up during the service, both services actually, and share her story. "Chad, the middle school pastor is the one speaking...he was wondering if you would be willing to share your story. It would be easy. He would just ask questions and you would answer."

"No! No way! Uh-uh!" Christina blurted out before Chris even finished proposing the idea.

There was conversation among the family about the gift it would be to the church to have Christina share. Christina didn't say much, having already made it clear how she felt about the whole thing. But, a deeper and firmer conversation was taking place in her heart.

*Will you follow Me Christina?*
*Lord, please, don't make me do this.*
*Will you follow Me Christina?*
*Yes Lord.*
*Then get up there and share your story.* The command was gentle.

*But you know I don't do this sort of thing.*
*I know YOU don't do this sort of thing. I do this sort of thing. Of course this isn't comfortable for you. But, that's why you need to rely on Me to give you the words, and to give you the courage.*

*But I'll probably just cry. And, Lord, You know I can't get a word out when I cry.*

*I love you Christina.*
*I can't do it Lord.*
*You can do all things through my strength.*
*Nobody wants to hear about little ol' me.*
*You have a story to tell that is very personal to you. By being*

168

*willing to share it, you have the opportunity to impact many lives with MY truth.*

*But I just need to do this whole cancer thing on my own Lord. This just gets complicated...bringing all these strangers into it.*

*This is part of why I created you.*

*But I don't want to be 'the cancer girl'...I just want to be normal. There's someone else with a better story Lord; someone who will be better at sharing it. Someone You can use more.*

*Christina, your story is really about Me, not you. You need to be willing to share it with others...otherwise it will be wasted.*

Her family was still discussing around her, but the decision was already made. Christina sighed. "Okay. I'll do it."

· · · · · · · · ·

Christina talked in front of a couple thousand people that Sunday. It was an occasion on par with a tornado as far as unlikely events go...or with a 25-year-old getting brain cancer, for that matter.

"Please make welcome Christina Ahmann."

The place erupted in applause, for many of these people had been praying for her over the last few months. Christina rose from her seat, her face hot, her buns tingling furiously. She willed herself to place one foot in front of the other, carefully directing them on how high to lift in mounting the stairs. She was grinning, but more from sheer terror than from joy at her reception. Chad put a hand on her arm when she came within reach and guided her to a stool.

"Thank you for being willing to be here and share your story Christina... I know it can be intimidating to stand in front of a large group like this."

Christina nodded, her eyes quickly scanning the room and noting the hundreds and hundreds of faces all looking right at her. Her buns tingled harder.

"But we are quite friendly."

Christina chuckled along with the congregation. She rocked back and forth from one leg to the other. She clasped her hands in front of her, then released them to hang at her side, then clasped them in front of her again. *Why do my arms feel so awkward in every position?*

"So, if you wouldn't mind first just outlining the circumstances that have led you to be here with us today."

169

Chad had a microphone in his hand that he then brought to Christina's face. Christina wasn't sure if she was supposed to grab it or not, so she spent a millisecond staring at its absorbent black orb. Chad looked at her expectantly, and that's when she realized that he already had a cordless mic wrapped around his ear and wobbling along his jaw line...so the microphone he held in her hand was indeed for her. She reached out and grabbed the handle.

"Um...well..." Christina was shocked at the enormity of the sound her voice made as it reverberated back to her through the monitors. *Is that really what I sound like?* I sound stuffed up. Buns tingling like crazy. Palms super sweaty on the metal handle. Face really hot. *Lord help.*

"Well, I guess...I guess the story really started last summer."

Chad nodded, encouraging her to go on when she looked at him. That's not enough of an answer, his look seemed to say.

It was "Mississippi Stop Stop" all over again. A pregnant pause, a questioning air in the audience, the silence, and then...

Chad gave her a simple nod and Christina did what she needed to do. She shared her story.

"See...God was really doing a lot in my heart that summer, preparing me for what was to come I guess."

She talked about those difficult summer months and her decision to surrender. Then she gave an abridged outline of the doctors' visits, the MRIs, the surgery and the radiation. At one point, the weepy stones of reminiscence lodged in Christina's throat and she couldn't speak without sounding like a sputtering jalopy. The congregation sat quietly for a moment. Then, in an act of solidarity with their sister, they started to clap. Christina chuckled through her tears and then finished her story.

"Obviously the Lord did amazing work in you before you even received a single diagnosis," Chad said. "Is there anything through the actual cancer journey that continued to affirm the Lord's presence with you?"

"Well..." Christina said slowly, forcing her brain to concentrate on the question and formulate an answer. It took but a second. "...yes, actually...something that really stood out to me and to everybody who walked this journey with me was the very real presence of God's peace. The Bible talks about His peace that passes all understanding, and I can vouch for that being a very real thing. It doesn't make a lot of sense that I and my family would be so peaceful through the diagnosis, the surgery, and all of it. But it was so apparent to us all that He was providing a very real and tangible peace for us. We would never have imagined ourselves to be so calm through a scary journey like that. But there we were. We would be smiling in appointments, and doctors would be looking at us all skeptical like, 'do you really understand what I'm telling you,' and we'd be like, 'we get it, we get it.' It didn't make sense, but we just felt so peaceful. And it had nothing to do with our spiritual maturity, or perfect prayers, or anything like that. We just needed peace, and God gave it to us because we needed it and we're His children. And how cool is that? God was just there, almost surrounding us in a bubble of peace, protecting us. His peace is not a floating thought that sounds nice and all…it's very real. And a lot of it, I firmly believe came from the many prayers of all the people out there, like you guys, who I know were praying so much for us. So thank you all for that."

Chad was nodding through her sharing. He quietly said 'Amen,' then said, "Well, as you heard, we talked about thankfulness today. Can you tell us what you've been particularly thankful for through this journey?"

"Well…I'm very thankful for my family. For a believing family that could walk through this with me in a way that I know a lot of other people in my situation do not get from their families. All my family: parents, brother and sister-in-law, cousins, aunts, uncles, they've all been so good to me…and my spiritual family…all you guys." Christina's arm passed through the air, making a sweep over all the heads facing her.

"I'm also thankful for Wesley, an incredible man who has entered my life through this journey. So unexpected, but so awesome."

Christina saw Wesley flash her an encouraging smile.

"Um…" Christina racked her brain for another coherent thought. "…I guess, I'm also really thankful for the many things that went well in this experience for me, that did not have to go well: having a great surgery, having excellent care, getting a wonderful house in Seattle to stay in while we do treatment, so much love from friends and family and from the body of Christ. There was just so much that we were so thankful for. Yeah…God is good."

Chad nodded. "Well, thank you very much Christina for being here today, for sharing with us your experiences with the Lord, your thankfulness and love for Him. We are all grateful for you. We'd like to pray for you if that's all right."

Christina nodded, bowed her head and let the words of the family of God flow over her. Inwardly, she thanked the Lord that she had managed to get through the talk without fainting.

And the Lord was blessed.

• • • • • • • • •

It was Saturday, December 1st. Christina and Wesley were at Mandy's apartment (she was a teacher in Seattle). They were watching the Civil War: Oregon State University versus University of Oregon football teams. At half time, the three prepared to go out into the falling snow to test their skills with the pigskin. Mandy and Wesley donned beanies. Christina already had one on, since she wore one almost all the time these days. They all wrapped up in big puffy coats, warm mittens and scarves.

There was much tugging and tagging and very little actual football that happened that afternoon on the small section of street in front of Mandy's apartment. The ground had a thin white blanket of snow that did little to pad the occasional fall one of them would take. Big wet snowflakes would land on their cheeks, melting quickly and forming little beads of numbness on their smiles.

It was the first significant amount of time that Christina spent without a thought about cancer…even forgetting she had it.

After they tumbled back into the house, breathless and frigid, they poured themselves mugs of hot chocolate and removed their outer layers.

As Wesley and Mandy pulled off their beanies, Mandy looked over at Christina. Christina smiled warmly at her friend, knowing what she was thinking.

"Can I see?" Mandy asked.

Christina shrugged her shoulders. "Sure." She reached up and gently pulled the beanie off her head.

Mandy stared at Christina's head.

Feeling the need to explain what was so visually clear, Christina said, "The wisps don't really cover it anymore. It's quite silly really to even pretend that they might."

Mandy grabbed one of the wisps. She lifted it to reveal the smooth shiny surface of Christina's scalp. Wesley brought Christina her mug of cocoa, smiling encouragingly at her. "I love the bald

172

spots," he said. "They make me think of my grandpa."

"Oh good. I look like a grandpa," Christina said sarcastically.

"I meant that as a compliment. I loved my grandpa. The warmth I have for him, is the warmth I feel about your bald spots."

Mandy was still fondling the wisps.

Christina tried to peek around her own head to get a glimpse of her friend's face. "I'm really close to just shaving it off. It's almost not worth it any more. What do you think?"

From behind her Christina quickly heard, "Do it!" Mandy's face followed her words, and her look was ecstatic. "Do it now!"

"Yeah!" Wesley joined in. "You should just shave it!"

"Shave it!" Mandy shouted, taking up a cheer.

"Shave it!" Wesley yelled. "And I'm shaving mine too!"

Christina was surprised at their enthusiasm. But it quickly overwhelmed her also. "Well, all right then. Let's shave it off."

"Yeah. Let's go!"

They threw all their soggy winter clothes back on and paraded out to Christina's car. They drove to the nearest SuperCuts, groaning when they saw it was closed.

"We'll buy clippers and do it ourselves," Mandy shouted, still in cheer mode.

They bought a buzzer at RiteAid and made their way back to Mandy's apartment.

In the kitchen, Christina held a mirror before her face, staring at her hair for the last time. She didn't feel any sense of sorrow about taking it off. She was actually really enthusiastic.

She plugged the razor in. It clicked to life and started to vibrate in her hand with a buzz. She set the metal edge against her forehead and, with a squeal ran it slowly through the brown folds of hair on top of her head.

Wesley and Mandy cheered loudly at the pokey airstrip that materialized out of Christina's hair.

Christina laughed. "Should I leave it like that?"

"Yeah right."

"Anybody else want to do a stripe?"

"Me, me, me," Mandy shouted, jumping up with a hand in the air.

"Go for it."

Mandy went at the right side of Christina's head with gusto, riding gently but firmly over the four bald spots Christina had been trying to hide for a couple weeks now. Each clump of hair that detached from her head and fell to the floor felt like a load falling off Christina's mind.

Wesley went next, tenderly removing the remaining half of Christina's hair, leaving a mown field of brown on the outline of her head. Christina grinned through the whole thing, praising God that this moment was feeling so perfect.

The buzzer clicked off, leaving a humming silence in the room. Wesley and Mandy waited for Christina's reaction. She studied herself in the mirror, turning her head this way and that. On the right side there were shiny bald patches, like burn sites on her scalp. The other side looked biker chic.

"I love it. GI Jane is here! Beware!"

"Yeah!" her fans cheered.

"Now come the one-handed push-ups!" Christina dropped immediately to the floor and, using both her arms, raised her body into a plank above the floor. She tried to release her left arm's support and hold herself up with only her right, but she promptly plopped to the floor. "Gonna have to work on that a bit more," she said.

Wesley and Mandy clapped at her effort.

"Who's next?" Christina asked, standing up.

"That would be me," Wesley said with a swagger. He grabbed the razor, raised it, then paused. "Would you please do the honors?" he asked, holding the razor out for Christina again.

"Gladly."

Twenty minutes later, Mandy was nodding approvingly at the stylish couple. "Awesome. You guys look hot."

"What about you Mandy?" Christina teased.

"I wish. But I think I would scare my students if I shaved my head. I'm joining you in spirit Christina."

"I know, I know. I'm joking. Thanks for nudging me to do this. I'm so happy."

"Of course. I'm just glad you're happy about it and not sad that I made you do it."

"Not at all. This was perfect." Christina looked over at Wesley, who grinned out at her from his shorn head. "And you look particularly handsome with a shaved head."

"Of course I do. But not as good as you look."

As they hugged, she whispered her thanks into his ear.

. . . . . . . . .

"Do you have everything?" Doug asked, his hand on the door to the House of Strength and Courage.

"I think so." Christina stood in the living room, her purse slung over her shoulder, her eyes scanning the living spaces of the house. JoDee emerged from the bedroom, her purse also slung over her shoulder. Her face was a blend of sadness and relief. She came and stood next to Christina. They both looked around, memories of the last 7 weeks in that house passing through their minds like happy home movies. It was December 11th: Christina's last day of treatment...their last day in Seattle.

"Well then?" JoDee said.

"Well then," Christina echoed.

Mother and daughter turned and headed out the door. Christina walked to her Ford, Doug and JoDee walked to their Toyota RAV4. They all stood a moment in the driveway. Then JoDee quickly strode over to Christina's car, opening the passenger door. "I'll just join you one last time to the hospital."

"Okay," Christina said, glad for company for her very last trip to the UW.

Doug smiled understandingly. "I'll see you both there then."

The ten minute drive was the same as it had been the last 32 times they had driven it. JoDee sat silent. Then, as if feeling a sudden urgency, she blurted, "Are you sure you don't want us to go back to Portland with you? Just to make sure you're feeling all right once you get back...settle in okay...and stuff?"

Christina smiled reassuringly at her mom. "Mom, I'm really okay. I really am. If you guys want to come, you can. But I'm okay."

"Well...I don't need to come just to make myself feel better," JoDee said. *But I want to.*

"Who would have thought that I would feel so great after 7 weeks of radiation?" Christina said.

"Who would have thought?" JoDee repeated, still contemplating whether she was going to tell Doug that they would be stopping in Portland on their way back to Port Angeles. "I really thought you would need a good spell to recover once you wrapped up here. I thought you might want to come to PA for a while...rest up...recover...you know."

175

"So did I."

"But clearly, you're fine."

"I'm fine." Christina watched her mom for a moment while they sat at a red light. "Are you fine?"

JoDee smiled at her daughter, finally deciding that she would go back to her life in PA. "I'll be fine."

"You can call me anytime."

"I know. And I will."

"It'll be weird. We've been together almost every day for the last 3 ½ months."

"I know," JoDee said heavily, thinking not of the last 3 ½ months, but of the next 3 ½ months.

"I'm surprised we're not sick of each other."

JoDee shook her head.

"Besides, I'll be up for Christmas in just about a week," Christina said.

"Oh, I know Christina. This is good. You're healthy, strong...you have energy. You need to go back to your life in Portland. You need to have some normalcy. You need to go to church, be a friend, be a girlfriend... without your parents putting their noses into everything you're doing. This is good. You go be normal." *Lord, please, please let her be normal for a LONG time. Please Lord.*

Christina spent her last ten minutes in the radiation therapy room, still cheering on her hair follicles in the hopes that they might miraculously produce hair again once this was all over, might pull a Lazarus. Therapists hugged the girl who had come in every day with a smile on her face...who brought smiles to their faces every day.

One of them suggested that she should be the face for radiation therapy at the UW Medical Center. "Come have radiation here. It's a breeze."

Christina and JoDee laughed at the joke, making sure to mention their strong belief that the "It's a breeze" part was because of the many people who had been praying for her through the treatment.

They had already had their last meeting with Dr. Ramsey. He had hashed through all the possible paths they might be taking after her next MRI in a couple weeks. The only reason they would be seeing him again would be with recurrence. She had been warned that it was possible her tumor was already rapidly filling in the gap

176

left from her surgery. In the case of recurrence, they discussed more surgery, chemo, gamma knife, radiation implants, everything.

The Ahmann family prayed fervently that the Lord would grant them a reprieve after this long stretch of medical minestrone.

After all the goodbyes, Christina walked out to her car with her family. They stood around for a moment, hesitant to separate. Finally JoDee stepped forward and hugged her daughter tightly. Doug gave her a long tender hug also. Then Christina got into her car, started the engine and, with boisterous waves to her parents, drove out of the parking lot. They stood and watched her a moment before getting in the car themselves. JoDee sighed heavily.

"You okay?" Doug asked.

JoDee paused. Of all the goodbyes she had planned to make as a mother: first day of school, summer camp, college…this goodbye was one for which she had not been prepared.

"I *will* be okay."

She spent the car ride planning how to get busy when she got home. By the time they hit PA, she had a nice effective list of chores to do, people to call, life to live.

· · · · · · · · ·

Christina got back to Portland on the 11th of December, happy…elated.

She wasn't sure how long her stay would be, but she knew she wanted to be back at home for at least a few days before she got another medical verdict. Normal life had never been so exciting before.

She unpacked her things. Her room was exactly as she had left it, cozy and comforting. Linsey was exactly as she had left her, bubbly and wonderful. Portland was busy, just like always.

But, she wasn't the same as she had always been. Her journey had changed her…permanently.

She had become a baldy with a life expectancy, an uncertain future, and a crazy past…all at 25 years old. And suddenly, she wasn't sure what life in Portland was supposed to look like anymore.

She found herself facing down a familiar feeling of inadequacy within the first few days of being home.

"So, are you working again?" It was one of the first things people would ask her once they saw her smiling and being herself. She figured it was one of the safest questions they could think of, as opposed to "So, how you feel about having brain cancer?" Work questions were easier. "You back at work?"

She felt like she was a disappointment when she would say, "No."

"What did you do today?" That was another one she got asked a lot. Linsey would ask her, Wesley would ask her, friends and people of no particular consequence would ask her. But no matter who asked the question, Christina always found herself trying to justify that she had spent all day unpacking, or writing emails, or catching up with friends in between rests. She didn't necessarily tell them that a task such as cleaning her room took several hours, an enormous amount of energy, all her brainpower, and always required a nap afterwards. She didn't tell them that she was actually very proud of herself for having accomplished that one thing in the day.

Christina started to feel very useless.

*Where do I fit in life now?*

*Where does my worth come from, if I don't work, if I don't accomplish anything in a day?*

*I should be more productive so I have something to tell people when they ask.*

These feelings were so familiar.

· · · · · · · · ·

Linsey walked in the door, humming. "Don't!"

Christina sat up straighter on the couch, where she had been watching TV. Fatigue had set in a couple hours ago. She had sat down wondering if her tumor was back, and had promptly fallen asleep. When she awoke, she had decided to veg out a while. "Don't."

"Watcha doin'?"

"Nothing." Of course, nothing.

"Wanna go to the store with me?"

Christina clicked off the remote. "Sure."

"I'm having Robbie over for a special dinner on Friday, and I need s'plies."

"Oh, I guess I should make sure to be at Wesley's on Friday then, huh?" Christina wasn't sure, but something about Linsey's need to have her away, bothered her.

"Well, it's fine if you guys are around. We might just go out after dinner or something. We haven't had any alone time in a

178

while."

"I'll tell Wesley we need to be at his house, don't worry. We'll give you guys some space."

"All right, thanks."

Christina went to the bathroom to straighten up, bothered by the feeling that she was in the way. She felt in Linsey's way. She even felt a little bit in Wesley's way. She felt like she was just hanging around all these people, with no reason for being there. *Or maybe that's just what I'm worried they're thinking about me.*

"Let's be off then," Linsey said, her purse over her shoulder, her stance eager. "Coffee first?"

"Uh, you know I still don't have much money -."

"My treat," Linsey interrupted.

"Linsey, we're back to the same old mooching thing."

"Christina, it's not mooching, so get over it. Let's go."

Christina grabbed her purse and followed Linsey outside. This whole scenario was painfully reminiscent: Linsey treating her to coffee, perpetual fatigue, feeling a sense of uselessness. And though it made no sense to her at all, Christina felt lonely.

She folded into the passenger seat, placed a CD into the player.

Lord, what's wrong with me now? Here I am, exactly where I asked to be: back in Portland, back to normalcy. And I'm sad, I'm lonely, I'm stuck in something other than the peace I knew with You.

And without even a word from the Spirit, Christina knew what was wrong with her. She had taken her eyes off of God. The drama of the cancer journey had paused...the drama that had made it easy to keep her focus on the Lord. Now, in the humdrum, the ordinary, the normal, Christina had forgotten to actively and passionately root herself in Christ. Cancer or no cancer, she still needed to do all things through the Lord's perfect strength. She couldn't seek her worth from work, from being useful, from Linsey, from Wesley...only from God.

The song blasting through the speakers was one of her favorite worship tunes. She started to sing along with it, feeling tears well up in her eyes, as they so often did these days.

Linsey sang with her and Christina let that car ride be her own personal worship service where she got to surrender, again.

· · · · · · · · ·

Christina was in the car with Wesley, on a journey to a

mysterious destination. Wesley had a continual smile on his face, knowing himself where they were headed, and loving that Christina didn't. It was a few days before Christmas and they were on Highway 2, headed east.

"This is pretty exciting. I love surprises."

Wesley grinned wider. "I love surprising."

"I wonder where we're going to land," Christina said in a little girl voice.

"You'll have to wait and see."

A few moments later, Christina said, also in a little girl voice, "Are we there yet?"

"Every turn of the wheel gets us a little bit closer."

"Well turn the wheels faster then."

"What... aren't you enjoying the car ride? The company?"

"Of course. I just wanna know."

Wesley raised his eyebrows. "Patience my dear."

"Well, you better talk to me then, keep me distracted so I don't focus on my impatience."

"What do you want to talk about?"

"I don't know. What do you want to talk about?"

"You're the one who needs the distraction. You pick the conversation."

"Okay. What's your favorite Christmas memory?"

They shared memories as they mounted Stevens Pass, driving slowly over the candy-coating ice on the roads. Conversation passed into silence in their descent. A CD of worship, the Tumor Mix as Christina called them, for it was full of songs she had listened to throughout her journey, looped repeatedly over the speakers. Christina hummed along, enjoying the view of whitewashed forests standing at attention on the sloping hills, an audience on their feet in honor of The Great Creator.

Finally Wesley broke into Christina's humming.

"When's your MRI?"

"December 27th. Why?"

"Just wondering."

"The follow-up appointment is January 4th."

"And you go up to Seattle for those, yes?"

"Yeah, but the MRI is done in Port Angeles this time."

"Right."

"You want to come to the appointment in Seattle with me? I

think it's a Friday."

"I don't know," Wesley hedged. "I'll have to check my work schedule. I'm taking a bunch of time off these couple weeks for the holidays, you know."

"Of course. It's not a big deal." Christina realized that if Wesley didn't come up to Seattle, it would be the first time he declined an opportunity to go there with her. But she understood. It wasn't the weekend. It was a workday. He couldn't go to everything with her.

Silence again. The grin Wesley had been wearing since yesterday had disappeared.

"What's going on?" Christina asked. "Is something bothering you?"

"No," Wesley said quickly. Too quickly.

"It's okay if something's bothering you, ya know. You can talk to me about it. I've always said that you don't have to put a brave face on all the time for me."

Wesley shook his head. "I'm not putting on a brave face for you."

"Well, your face doesn't look very happy right now, that's for sure," Christina said, attempting a little levity.

Wesley passed a smile over at her. Then he looked back at the road and said nothing.

"Are you starting to get stressed about this whole cancer thing?...having doubts?"

Wesley sighed, seeming to contemplate whether or not he wanted to talk about it. Then he sighed again and said, "Yeah, I think I might be having doubts."

Christina almost felt a sense of relief. He was human after all. She was thrilled at the opportunity to finally be able to hash out some of his emotions.

"Doubts about what specifically? The unknown future? The shadow of cancer?" She paused. Without thinking about it, she said, "Us?"

Wesley sort of shook his head. Then he almost mumbled, "Just... everything."

Her elation of a moment before quickly evaporated. "Okaaay. Do you want to talk about it?"

"I'm not sure what there is to talk about. I don't really know what my doubts are about yet. I'll let you know if something becomes clear, but it's not like there's something that's bothering me and I need to straighten it out on this car ride, ya know."

"Okaaay." Christina stared out the front windshield. The trees still stood at attention before the Lord, but now, she somehow felt left out of their community.

"What about you?" Wesley said, seeming to try to shift attention from his emotions to hers. "How are you feeling about the upcoming MRI?"

"Ummm," Christina struggled to shift gears. The insecurity that their brief words had created within her spirit were clouding her conversational intelligence. "Well, you know, it's hard knowing that the MRI could show the tumor has grown back to practically the same size or whatever. It's tough to think that after radiation, I'll just move right on to the next treatment...no break."

"Uh-huh."

Christina decided to let go of the fears that had sheathed her soul a moment earlier and go back to a trusting spirit. She dove into the topic. "Actually, I was thinking about it the other day. I've had this past week in Portland to live my life like I used to, you know. And like, within a day of being back, I found that I wasn't seeking God with the fervency that I've had to this whole past year. I definitely began to coast spiritually...tried to live on my own strength, ya know. Well, very quickly I found myself consumed by a flood of emotions: fear, hopelessness, insecurity, annoyance, acute self-awareness. It was gross. And it was shocking how quickly it took over when I thought I could do it without the Lord. So, it got me thinking about how that's not how I'm supposed to live my life...that's not how any of us are supposed to live our lives. We're supposed to find our fullness in Christ...nothing else can satisfy. So, it made me realize it could be a blessing in some ways to live from one MRI to the next. Let's say this one comes back with a really positive outlook. Well, I'll just have another one in three months that could be negative for all I'd know. It's like, every three months I get to be reminded...no, forced, to let everything go again...to surrender my life, my family, my relationships, my dreams...give them all to God. That seems like a really good way to live doesn't it? We all should be so privileged to have a constant reminder that we need to live here and now...with intensity...with purpose."

Wesley made no comment at first. He squinted his eyes as he stared at the road. Christina watched him, wondering what he was thinking.

Then he said, "Well, maybe not all people would see it as a blessing to live from one MRI to the next. Maybe...maybe you're just blessed that you can have such a positive outlook about it."

Christina felt her heart leap into her throat, as if Wesley had just driven off a cliff and all her organs missed out on the warning. This kind of talk had never come out of Wesley's mouth before. He was always the first to join in her enthusiasm about what God was revealing to her through this journey.

As difficult as it was to talk with a heart pounding rapidly in her throat, she felt the need for immediate clarification. "I'm not special. My outlook is all because of the Lord." Her words came out harsher than she intended, but it was hard to sugarcoat the need she felt to defend her state of mind and the glory of God's goodness.

Wesley just shrugged his shoulders.

Christina stared forward. The Tumor Tunes had started over from the very beginning.

They rode quietly, almost sullenly for a little while.

Before long, Christina reached out with an olive branch of conversation again and Wesley accepted it. They chatted lightly until they hit the town of Leavenworth, nestled in the Cascades.

This was the surprise. Wesley grinned like a schoolboy again as they took a sleigh ride through the snowy swells outside of Leavenworth. They laughed and snuggled and it felt like it always had between them. After the sleigh ride, in the trip Leavenworth up to Port Angeles, conversation remained upbeat.

Christina tried to put her unease aside and accept the moments as they were.

. . . . . . . . .

It was Thursday night...the night before she and Linsey would drive up to Seattle to visit with Dr. Thompson to get the results of her MRI.

Christina sat in her room at Pettygrove Lane. Her eyes felt heavy, loaded with liquid. Her Bible lay open on her lap. It was late. Wesley had already left for home. He wouldn't be able to accompany her tomorrow, but he had been very encouraging tonight.

She should be asleep by now. She could tell by the heavy silence that seemed to bump against her bedroom door that Linsey was already slumbering. But Christina just sat on her bed, her lamp shedding a cone of light over her bed, her legs, and the Bible.

The reservoir of tears was pressing against her eyelids.

*Am I enough Christina? Will you go with Me?*

The questions were always the same. And every time she devised her answers, Christina had to examine her heart...delve into the depths of the soul...mine it for resistance...make sure her answers were sincere.

These conversations with the Lord were a lot like massage visits. Christina would see a client, work out tight fibers, push out the toxins, warm up the muscles, release the nerve fibers from obstructions. But one visit would only last so long. Life would fight back. Muscles would tighten again. Tension would build. Stiffness would set in. Time for another massage.

Her last surrender to the Lord would be sincere, but it wouldn't take long for fear, doubt, pity, to whet their teeth on the softness of Christina's heart, creating ragged edges, building hardened walls between her and the Lord. Time to surrender again.

*Lord, I like being back here, not at the hospital.*

*Am I enough?*

Some tears eased out the corners of her eyes. *Absolutely Lord. But I really like Wesley. I can picture a life with him. It feels really good.*

*Will you follow Me and let Me worry about Wesley?*

More tears. *Yes Lord. But could You spare him and spare my family from any pain that tomorrow's news might bring.*

*Can you give Me Wesley? Can you give Me your family? Do you trust Me to care for them?*

Lots of tears, as Christina imagined her parents hearing news tomorrow that might involve the death of their daughter.

*Yes Lord. Your Love for them is greater than mine. I give them all to You.*

Christina wiped her nose on a tissue. She read from the Psalms. She prayed fervently. Then she lay down, her Bible still open on her chest. She turned off the light, and fell asleep.

· · · · · · · · ·

JoDee and Christina sat next to each other in the small room. They were both aware that they had been in that very same posture so many times over the last 4 months: side by side, waiting for news.

They didn't say much as they waited.

184

Finally, the door knob turned and in walked Dr. Thompson, his face warm and friendly.

"Hello Christina," he said. "JoDee."

They greeted him, smiling as they always had, though with a tinge of fatigue this time.

"Well," Dr. Thompson said, sitting down in his high-backed cushioned seat. He shook his head. "Your brain looks beautific."

JoDee brought her head forward, questions lining her face. Christina just smiled.

"'Beautific?' What exactly does that mean?" JoDee asked, wondering if 'beautific' was even a word.

"Well," Dr. Thompson said, slightly shaking his head, "it means that your brain looks beautiful. There is no sign of cancer or of a tumor or of damage in your brain, except a nice hole where the tumor used to be."

JoDee and Christina's mouths both dropped open. This sentence from Dr. Thompson was not at all something they had planned on hearing. They were prepared for ambiguity to be the main theme of their visit. They had been repeatedly told that post-radiation MRIs were difficult to read and usually necessitated return visits, further tests, more analysis. They had also prepared for the bad news, the mediocre news, even the slightly good news.

What they had not prepared for, was the miraculous news.

They asked a thousand questions...most of them about the possibilities of recurrence from this point on.

Dr. Thompson finally laughed and said, "You guys are awfully focused on a recurrence that hasn't even happened yet. I just told you wonderful news and all you want to know about is the possibility of its return."

JoDee and Christina looked at each other and chuckled. Then JoDee said, "Well, it's not too often you get a full audience with your doctors, so we try to take every opportunity to get as many answers as possible...to be prepared, you know."

"I understand," Dr. Thompson said gently. "But, I'm telling you, your MRI looks great."

"Can we see it?" Christina asked impulsively.

Dr. Thompson looked slightly taken aback. Then he shrugged his shoulders. "Sure. Why not?"

He led them to a darkened room. They stood before a computer while he found their file. He pulled up the photo and they all stared in awe at Christina's brain. What a marked difference from this scan to the one they had looked at in Dr. Crowley's office four months before. It looked like a brain...a brain with a small gap in the right corner.

"Wow!" Christina said.

"Exactly what I was thinking," JoDee said.

"Mmm-hmmm," Dr. Thompson said quietly, letting mother and daughter enjoy the evidence of God's work for a moment.

"But the cancer is still in there right?" Christina asked.

Dr. Thompson frowned, staring at the brain. "Well, theoretically, yes. Your type of tumor infiltrates into the surrounding brain tissue, so it's impossible to remove all the cancer tissue without damaging the brain." Dr. Thompson's fingers of his right hand spread out like infiltrating cancer tendrils. "But, there's no sign of necropsy, decay of brain tissue from the cancer." He pointed to the beautific brain.

"So..." JoDee started, unsure of what to ask, but needing more.

"Statistically speaking," Dr. Thompson offered, "90% of Christina's type of tumor come back, usually in a more aggressive form." He shrugged his shoulders. "But we can't say anything for sure. Time will tell."

Christina was still staring at the picture of her brain. A small white patch in the corner was all that remained of her serpent; a worn down patch where it had been nestled. The spot could be ominous if she thought about what might be hiding along its edges; branches weaving into her brain, trails slithering through her thoughts. But she chose not to dwell on it. Today she would rejoice.

Dr. Thompson sent them on their way with handshakes and a promise to reconvene in three months.

JoDee and Christina walked arm in arm to the waiting room where Tammy and Linsey sat, hands clenching armrest, feet bouncing nervously, trapped under the veil of déjà vu. Mother and daughter squealed as they saw their friends. JoDee let Christina say the words: "My brain is beautific!"

Linsey and Tammy stood up quickly, their faces confused, also wondering what 'beautific' meant.

JoDee clarified. "There is no visible sign of a tumor!"

Hugs. Tears. Squeals. More hugs. Prayers of thanksgiving and praise.

On the way out of the hospital, Christina jumped high up into the air, clapping her feet together with Gene Kelly precision. JoDee captured the moment on film.

. . . . . . . . .

Christina went back to Portland after that day of fabulous news, looking to settle in for a good spell this time. She quickly reconnected into her networks: touching base with her high school girls, thanking every church person that she came across for their support of her and her family, stopping by the chiropractor's office where they told her she was welcome back any time she was ready.

She spent a lot of time with Linsey, being the roommate she had wanted to be last summer but had been unable to because of her fight against death. And now, the urgency to be good roommates was made more poignant by the nearness of its cessation, for Linsey and Robbie had gotten engaged in February and were to be married in March. The two girls were determined to enjoy the last few pages of their chapter as roommates.

She made a couple trips to PA, visiting her parents, speaking at her old church.

Life was good...for the most part.

. . . . . . . . .

Ever since she had returned to Portland, Christina struggled to understand how to be a normal girlfriend to this man who had been a vital part of her spiritual journey through brain cancer. Now that brain cancer had become simply a facet of her life, rather than the definition, the two of them were in limbo. Christina was sensing a withdrawal. She was very forgiving through it. Dating brain cancer would be hard on any guy. Maybe he was finally facing up to the reality of it.

What she tried to ignore was the whisper in the back of her mind that maybe dating brain cancer had been the excitement in the relationship. Now that the intensity was gone, maybe the relationship was missing its foundation. Christina worked hard to reestablish the base that she thought they had built over the last several months...she fought for the relationship. But it didn't take long for her to realize that she was fighting alone.

It was Valentine's Day... that day for dating couples.

But Christina felt none of the joy most dating girls would on this day. She was coming to grips with the fact that the relationship she and Wesley had was not good enough. It had to change or it wouldn't work. The man had stopped showing up when he knocked on her door. He would be a person on the couch next to her when they watched a movie or a body across the table from her while they shared a meal, but the heart was absent. She would try to engage him, try to interest him, try to remind him of where they had been. But to no avail.

Wesley had called an hour ago. He was on his way to bring her a Valentine gift. He had thanked her for the card she had left on his truck at work earlier in the day. Christina knew the card she had made him had been nothing to crow about. She couldn't conjure up some gushy love note just because it was Valentine's Day.

She was curious what his gift would be.

She sat at the kitchen table. Linsey was out with Robbie. The house reeked of loneliness.

A knock on the door. She pulled it open. Wesley stood on the porch, a small smile on his face…an empty smile.

"Hi," she said, trying to sound happy.

"Hey." He stepped into the living room. "I got you this." He handed her an envelope.

"Thanks." She opened it. It was a Hallmark Card, stating a stale verse of affection. In his own hand, Wesley had written about his appreciation of her. A gift card for Nordstrom's sat in a smaller envelope within the card. "Thanks."

"I thought you might need to get some new clothes or something."

"Thanks. That was very thoughtful of you." She reached up to hug him. As all his hugs had been lately, this one was rote.

Wesley sat down on the couch.

"What do you want to do tonight?" he asked, not looking in her eyes.

"Well, don't you want to go to Bible Study?" Christina asked slowly, sitting down next to him. She was wondering why they were even talking about this. They always went to Bible study on Thursday nights. Why wouldn't they tonight?

"I don't know," Wesley said with a casual shrug. "Do you want to go?"

Christina paused, every muscle in her body tensing. This was not good. She made a rash decision. "You know, why don't you just go alone tonight. I think I want to stay home."

Now Wesley did look in her eyes, almost with relief. Quickly he said, "That sounds good." He stood up, looking awkward. "In fact, maybe we should just take this weekend and spend some time apart. Think...be alone...ya know."

Christina wasn't surprised any more by the course this encounter was taking. She was hardening up to him. "That sounds fine." She stood next to him.

"Fine." Wesley reached out for a hug.

Christina slowly stepped into it, careful not to press too tightly against him.

"Happy Valentine's Day," Wesley said, pulling away and starting toward the door.

"Yeah." She watched him walk to his car. He looked back at her and flashed her a smile that for one brief moment looked like the old Wesley. She felt a sudden urge to run after that man. But she didn't.

She shut the door before he had left the driveway. She walked back to her bedroom and packed a bag.

. . . . . . . . .

The next Monday Christina sat in her room in PA. Her parents had given her space over the weekend, knowing things were not well with her and Wesley. She sat on the window seat, studying the raging wind that rushed up the Strait of Juan de Fuca, curling the water's surface into white crescents.

She knew that if things didn't change with Wesley, their relationship would have to end. She couldn't live this way anymore, pretending to be together with a person who walked ahead of her on their path, lost in his own thoughts, glancing occasionally back to see if she was still there. It wasn't enough for her.

But the thought of the relationship ending was fraught with emotion. Not only would it break her heart, but it would require a lot of explaining. Everybody knew about Wesley. He was all over her webpage, she had talked about him in all her little talks, all her supporters had fallen in love with him as much as she had. He had become the knight in shining armor, swooping into her story to carry off the cancer patient in strong arms of unexpected love.

Christina had to fight away the thoughts that teased her into believing for a moment that the chance to be the benevolent knight

189

was the whole reason he had lifted her into his arms in the first place. Christina shook her head, closed her eyes and tried to squeeze away her hurt.

Her phone rang. It was Wesley.

She picked it up and squeezed its plastic body in her fist. "Hey," she answered.

"Hey. How was your weekend?"

"It was all right. How was yours?"

"It was pretty good actually. Hey, I was wondering if you wanted to meet for lunch today…and talk."

"Well, I'm actually in PA."

"Oh." He was surprised.

"But I can talk now."

"Oh, well. Um. I just wanted to talk about us, ya know."

Christina braced herself. "What about us?"

"Well, I think it's time for us to move on."

Heat flowed through her body. It hurt more than she thought it would. "What?"

"Yeah. I think our relationship has run its course and we need to decide to be friends from here on out… move on."

"Move on."

"Yeah."

Christina fought the warming up of her tear ducts. "What do you mean our relationship has run its course? Do you not care about me any more?"

"Of course I care about you Christina. It's just that…I think…I think my affection for you is more like…"

*Please don't say 'like a sister.'*

"…more like a sister."

Christina hit the bed.

"A sister huh?"

"Yeah."

"So, you're just not into me as a girlfriend you're saying."

"Well, you know, I just don't think we're a match."

"And we never were?... or you changed your mind?"

"I'm not sure. Sometimes I think it was really the Holy Spirit that I was attracted to in you, ya know. "

Christina cringed. Tears rolled down her cheeks at the insensitive words.

"Wesley. You really mean this…you're really just done with

this...after all we've been through?" She fought the quiver in her voice.

"Look, I'm sorry if this is shocking to you, but I really think we just need to move on."

*Yes, you've said that.*

Uncertain she could say anything else without breaking down into embarrassing sobs, Christina nodded against her cell. "Okay," she said softly.

"We can talk more when you get back if you want."

"So we're done?"

"Well, we can talk..."

"No it's okay."

"Okay, then. Call me when you get back."

"Okay."

"Bye."

"Bye." Her last syllable came out as a squeak. Her face was flush with heat, with shame, with embarrassment, with anger, with intense and drowning sorrow.

*Lord!!!*

*Christina. Remember...I asked if you could give Wesley to Me.*

*I know, but that's not what I meant.*

*I know.*

*But, Lord.*

*Am I enough Christina?*

"Yes Lord!" Christina sobbed.

A few minutes later, she emerged from her bedroom. She walked to the balcony overlooking the living room. JoDee was in the kitchen, but she was aware of her daughter's presence above her. She walked into visibility. She saw a tear-stained face, a crushed spirit.

"WHAT did he DO?!?"

. . . . . . . . .

After that phone call, Christina spent another day in Port Angeles, largely confined to her room. She sat at the window seat looking out over the strait, fervently praying.

These tears were heavier than any she had shed on her journey through brain cancer...they hurt more.

*Lord, I didn't ask for this relationship. Why did it even happen?*

No answer.

*I didn't want to get attached to someone at this time. But I did Lord. I fell in love. I trusted him. I let myself love. Did he even love me back Lord?*

Still no answer.

Christina thought through the whole relationship, beginning to end. It had felt so right, so sweet in the beginning. It had definitely soured by the end, but Christina's experience throughout had been pure. Her emotions had been genuine, her heart had been true.

*What am I supposed to learn through this Lord? Do I still need to learn something? Is there something I haven't given You? I thought I had given You Wesley...did I not really? Did I make it through cancer only to lose my heart to a man?*

*Christina, there is nothing new under the sun. Through every obstacle, every problem, the question is still the same: Will you follow Me?*

Christina pulled out her Bible.

2 Corinthians 4:16-18

> "Therefore we do not lose heart. Though outwardly we are wasting away, yet inwardly we are being renewed day by day. For our light and momentary troubles are achieving for us an eternal glory that far outweighs them all. SO WE FIX OUR EYES NOT ON WHAT IS SEEN, BUT ON WHAT IS UNSEEN. For what is seen is temporary, but what is unseen is eternal."

*Yes Lord. I will follow You.*

Christina sat down and composed a letter to Wesley outlining her hurt and releasing her frustration. It was a healing move. She relinquished expectations, hopes and fears, letting God having every last piece of her again.

After she folded it up and put it in an envelope, Christina immediately felt better. The despair was gone, and God's peace was back.

She was ready to move on, staff in hand.

# The Sparrow

*It can be easy to be overwhelmed with all the 'unknowns' that come with so many changes, but God has put overwhelming peace in my heart that He most definitely has a specific plan for me and wants me to get as excited as He is for the new adventures just around the corner.  I serve a most creative God who intricately weaves my journey (as well as yours) into tapestries of beauty...the kind of beauty that lets difficulties, tears, blessings, and joys, equally add to the breathtaking character of our life witness.*

*Love,*

*Christina*

Exodus 6:1

Then the Lord said to Moses,
  "Now you will see what I will do."

# After it all...

So, you have brain cancer. In all likelihood, as statistics go at least, the tumor will return, quite aggressively. Life becomes one three-month journey at a time: years pieced together by precious segments.

What do you do? How do you fill three months, always conscious of the possibility that the 'normalcy' with which you pass the days could be over in the time it takes to click on a light switch behind a brain scan.

These were the challenges with which Christina passed through the year of 2008. And on top of the somber awareness of her new reality, there was the heartbreak of the relationship ending, a major lesson for Christina to again surrender all to the Lord.

But Christina did not pass this year in sorrow. Her many 'surrendering visits' with the Lord had taught her that no matter her circumstances, her joy was to be found in God. And she decided to live her life with joy, three months at a time: savoring each and every relationship, old and new; diving into the deep end in all conversations; laughing hard at every joke and prank; napping wholeheartedly, eating with gusto, loving with purpose.

There truly was a lot of joy. Linsey and Robbie got married, an event for which Christina got a front row seat in her role as maid of honor. With the loss of her best roommate, Christina moved into a new house with a new girl, and formed a new friendship. She went on a trip to Hawaii with her family. And even as she worked to maintain old relationships with friends, she found that there were many opportunities for new relationships with kindred spirits whose bodies also carried some reminders of a run-in with Death. Christina embraced these relationships wholeheartedly, loving the immediate intimacy that their shared experiences offered.

And her hair grew back! The shiny bald spots she had been told to hold out no hope for began to shrink as wisps of hair began to convene, making the shine smaller and smaller every week.

Christina continued to strive to do bold things. She gave talks whenever asked. Though never did she grow accustomed to being put in the spotlight; her buns still tingled and her laughter through the microphone still rang with nerves. But she pursued the courageous choice, trusting the Lord to give her the strength to do what did not come naturally to her.

She continued to update her web page, keeping people apprised of the many joys and, quite candidly, describing her fears and challenges as well. She publicly lived out her life for the benefit of others.

And work... Work? It didn't take long after radiation treatments for Christina to start contemplating what she was going to do to earn a living again. Up to this point, she had been subsisting under the generous wing of her parent's support. But she couldn't do that forever. The main inhibitor to Christina's career was fatigue. Each day's energy level was severely tempered by her history. Brain surgery, even a good one, leaves a footprint. Radiation, an even bigger one.

After taking courses to reactivate her license, Christina started working days again at the chiropractor's office in the spring of 2009. Walking into work that first day felt strange to Christina. Her last time working there had been in a different lifetime. That day she had not been able to read the white writing on the black hat.

She was scheduled for just half the day...the idea was to start slow...see how things went. She would see three clients.

Christina smoothed out the sheets on the massage table. She put Enya into the CD player.

She stood a moment, eyes scanning the dim room, reflecting on its tangible peacefulness. She wanted her life to always be like a ready massage room. Always ready for surrender, peaceful and welcoming.

She sighed and went out to the lobby, surprised at her nervousness... fresh-out-of-massage-school nervousness.

She called to her client, a middle-aged woman with severe whiplash. Christina talked with her about her symptoms. Then she left so the woman could undress.

Elda sat behind the reception desk, just like normal. The sitting room looked the same...but the new carpet smell was gone.

"It's so great to have you back Christina. I missed you and our talks."

"Thanks Elda!" Christina patted Elda's back, overwhelmed with affection. "It's great to be back. It really is. Though I have to confess, I'm a bit nervous about my first real massage."

Elda swatted at the air. "You'll do great. You always do. It's just like riding a bicycle...it all comes right back....I think."

Christina laughed. "Oh, Elda, do you know that you're the

best?"

"Oh!" Elda shook her head with a smile. "By the way, I scheduled your next client for two hours after this one, in case you need to take a nap in between."

Christina was overwhelmed again. "Seriously. Elda. You ARE the best! Thank you for looking out for me."

"Oh, sure." Elda went back to her typing, smiling at Christina's praise.

Christina reviewed her client's paperwork again, making sure she was aware of any sensitivities the woman may have in her pain. Her eyes landed on the word 'cancer.' It sat in an extensive list of conditions a massage therapist would need to be aware of in a client: low blood pressure, varicose veins, diabetes, cancer.

It was a strange confluence of two significant elements to Christina's life: her choices and her circumstances.

Cancer patients getting massage. She knew it happened all the time. A colleague of hers had come to her home a couple times to relieve some of the tension in her neck after her surgery. It had been fabulous.

*I should figure out how I can do massage for cancer patients.*

It was a simple, obvious revelation. It didn't hit her like a lightning bolt; more just a subtle 'note-to-self.'

But that seed of a thought would grow slowly and steadily over the next few months.

• • • • • • • • •

Gayle MacDonald. Christina had never heard the name before... but it was about to change her life.

That seed of a thought, 'oncology massage,' had been growing. Friends and family had encouraged Christina to make some calls, do some research.

There had been a course on oncology massage back in massage school. Christina had not taken it.

She called the school to pursue the possibility of auditing the class, or helping out with it...anything to be near it and glean whatever information she could.

The instructor told her about the class, its focus, its hours, its availability. Unfortunately, the class was on the one day a week Christina put in her hours at the chiropractor's office, a day that really could not change. But the instructor had given her the name that Christina now held in her hand.

She flipped open her laptop, fired up the Internet and typed in the name: 'Gayle MacDonald.'

The first hit was 'medicinehands.com.' Christina clicked on it and immediately was sucked into the site's descriptions about the value and importance of massage for cancer patients. Gayle MacDonald was a massage therapist and instructor who specialized in oncology massage. She had written a book called 'Medicine Hands' that outlined how massage could help cancer patients in their healing process. Christina took it all in, feeling the sprouts of purpose bursting forth in her soul.

She clicked on the schedule of classes for oncology massage instruction.

The next course Ms. MacDonald would be teaching in the area was that next weekend in Salem. After that, Ms. MacDonald would be off teaching in Scotland, then Minnesota, then all over the place. She wouldn't be back in the area again for another six months.

Christina called immediately and signed up.

The day of the class, apprehension preceded Christina into the meeting room. The room was full with an eclectic mix of people chatting in groups. A clump of women with dreadlocks and hemp skirts mingled near the door, pausing to smile pleasantly at Christina as she walked by. A mixed group of young people, probably about her age, sat in the lined chairs, exchanging career-start-up stories. An older group of people sat in chairs, leaning towards each other as they talked.

Christina sat down and worked her bottom lip with her upper teeth as she scanned the room.

Then, a middle-aged woman with short graying hair stood at the front of the room and introduced herself. Gayle MacDonald's face was rather serious, but would occasionally burst into an unexpected bright smile that put Christina at ease.

As an ice breaker, she wanted every person in the room to introduce him/herself and state their purpose in taking the course.

Christina sweated until it was her turn, debating ways to answer the question honestly without making herself 'the cancer girl.' But then she realized there was no reason to hide the truth. The courageous choice always involves the truth.

Someone to Christina's right was sharing. He was an older man with a trembling voice and a down-turned head. He was saying that he was not a massage therapist but was interested in oncology massage because his wife had cancer and he wanted to use massage to help her with her pain.

Ms. MacDonald nodded sympathetically.

Then the woman next to Christina shared. She was middle aged, with short brown hair, pointed upward in crunchy spikes.

"Hi, I'm Jenny. I *really* want to educate myself on massage for cancer patients. I've been giving massages for twenty years now and I come from the school of thought that massage is contraindicated in cancer patients…that's what we were taught in school. So, at my clinic I've had people come in for a session, and once I've seen that they've checked off cancer on their papers, I've sent them away." The woman shook her head in shame. "I've had clients burst into tears when I've told them I can't give them a massage."

Ms. MacDonald's face looked sad as she listened.

Jenny was looking down at her hands, seeming to collect herself to go on. "I've since become aware that a lot of massage therapists *do* give massages to cancer patients. And I really want to be one of them. I don't want to make another person cry needlessly like that again."

Ms. MacDonald nodded. "Thank you for sharing Jenny. One thing we'll talk about today is a patient's desire to do something normal, like get a massage… and when we've turned them away in the past, it just reminds them that they're not normal."

Jenny nodded soberly, close to tears.

"Thank you Jenny. We'll make sure you get the information you need today." Ms. MacDonald's eyes moved to Christina.

"Hi, I'm Christina." Buns tingling. "I've been a massage therapist for four years now. But I've been on a bit of a hiatus. Two years ago, I was diagnosed with brain cancer."

The room inhaled. Ms. MacDonald's eyes seemed to bore straight through Christina, right into her skull.

"I had surgery, and went through radiation treatment. I've had several clear MRIs and have been trying to get back into work. I remember hearing about oncology massage and I've been really longing to learn more about it. I want to be able to help cancer patients as they walk through their journeys. I've developed a passion for them, ya know."

The room was quiet. Some people were staring at her with sympathy. Others looked away with discomfort.

Ms. MacDonald's cheeks lifted suddenly, pulling her mouth into a warm smile. "Christina. Thank you so much for sharing. We're thrilled to have you here today. Having someone who has experience with cancer will be good for us...you can tell us if our information is correct."

Christina laughed. "Okay."

The rest of the class shared their names and purposes. Then Ms. MacDonald began her lecture.

"Skilled touch on a person's body can diminish pain, nervousness, anxiety, depression. As a patient relaxes more, his or her body can be more freed up to fight, heal, and rest." Ms. MacDonald glanced briefly at Christina with that last sentence. "Touch also brings back a sense that a patient's body can be a source of good feelings, not just bad. It can remind the patient that he or she is lovable, worthwhile. I've walked up to patients receiving chemotherapy treatments and everything about their face reflects distress. The minute I put my hands on them, sometimes I can actually see the muscles in their jaw and forehead let go and relax."

Ms. MacDonald described massage's benefits, combating old beliefs that massage was negative for a cancerous body.

"But, it is imperative that massage be done correctly, or it can cause great harm to the patient. It's not always the cancer itself that makes a patient susceptible to harm from a massage... the treatment that the patient is going through can make them particularly vulnerable, as well.

"Of course, each type of treatment has different effects on the body. Let's talk more specifically about what each treatment does to the body. Let's start with radiation."

Ms. MacDonald looked at Christina again. She walked through radiation and its effects on a patient's body. A few times, as she was describing the actual experience of getting radiation treatment she would pause, look at Christina and say, "Is that right?"

Christina would smile and nod her approval of Ms. MacDonald's descriptions. She never needed to add anything. She figured Ms. MacDonald mostly wanted to be sensitive to Christina's hands-on knowledge.

At the break, folks came up to Christina: to congratulate her, to welcome her back to the field, to share their own trials with her. Unlike some people, Christina did not find it irritating when people wanted to share their misfortunes with her because they perceived her to be an understanding soul. Christina *was* an understanding soul. Their perception that she would be a sympathetic listener was correct. She was happy to let her story be the conduit for better conversations with strangers.

After the conference, Christina felt encouraged in her pursuit of oncology massage.

· · · · · · · · ·

Over the next several months, the budding of Christina's passion blossomed into an all-out desire to pursue oncology massage with her life. She hooked up with a woman who ran an internship program at Oregon Health and Sciences University, OHSU, in the chemotherapy ward. Christina was one of four students in the program that fall of 2009. The course involved a weekend of training and instruction and then several months of visits to the hospital.

Christina took the elevator to the 7th floor of OHSU: the infusion floor. She walked slowly toward the nurse's station, feeling a mix of excitement and trepidation.

*Lord, I'm really excited about this. If this is Your plan for me Lord, just make it clear. Give me the strength. Give me the courage to approach people I don't know and introduce myself. Give me the physical strength to do this for three hours. Give me words of encouragement for the patients. Soften their hearts to receive tenderness and love from my touch, and, if they want it, encouragement and support from my words.*

*Lord, in all I do, may Your name be glorified.*

She walked up to the nurse's station and introduced herself.

"Hi. I'm Christina. I'm here for the oncology massage internship."

"Ah yes," one of the nurses said. Her friendly face immediately brought Christina back to the role of a brain cancer patient eager to soak up the warmth of her wonderful nurses. "I'm Shannon."

"Hi Shannon. Nice to meet you."

"You'll need this," Shannon said, handing Christina a badge that had her name over the title 'Massage Therapist.' "Whenever you do a shift, you'll need to sign in here." Christina wrote her name in a notebook. Shannon handed her a second notebook. "This notebook has all the patients' information in it. Before you give a massage you need to check their file. And after you're done, if you have anything to add, new symptoms, patients' complaints, you can add it here.

"If you have any questions about specific patients, don't hesitate to ask any of the nurses on the floor."

Christina nodded. "Okay."

"Okay then," Shannon smiled, then went off to tend to a patient.

Christina turned around and scanned the room. Though the setting was familiar to her, for she had visited this floor before in her training, it was still foreign. She had not had chemotherapy. She couldn't tap into a well of experience to make sense of the sounds and sights she now witnessed.

She followed the arc of the room. Each curtained section along the wall had a leather chair where a patient sat, arm on the arm rest, tube in flesh, liquid flowing. Various stages of baldness were represented: full heads of hair unaffected yet, sparkling pates of accepted bareness, bright colorful wigs, wispy dull strands of denial. The patients read, slept, chatted with family or friends, and watched movies on their laptops. Some faces were hardened by experience, some were ripe with fear and newness. Every face reflected many emotions.

Christina swallowed hard. *This could be me.*

She watched a mother try to make her child, an adult child, more comfortable. She gently lifted his bald head and placed it on a second pillow, smoothing out the edges next to his ears, as though to keep open his ability to hear her words of love and encouragement. His smile was weak, but thankful.

A heat behind her eyes, Christina thought, *This is me.*

She marched to the far corner of the room, praying for strength.

The first patient was laying back, eyes closed, ear buds in his ears. Christina stood a moment at his feet, unsure what to do. Even the offer of a massage hardly seemed a good enough reason to disturb a person's nap. She moved on. The next cubicle was firmly closed off by a curtain. Christina tapped gently on the white plastic sheet, voicing a soft 'hello' as she peeked into the space. A woman, worn past her years, stared at her through hollow eyes. The molded shape of her brow, where eyebrows would have been, pinched over her eyes and a questioning look pierced across the small space right into Christina's discomfort.

"Hi," Christina whispered. Her heart was pounding. "I'm

Christina. I'm a massage therapist and I was just wondering if you would like a complementary massage."

The woman glared. "No."

"Okay. Sorry to bother you." She quickly pulled back from the curtain, letting it fall together, forming a barrier to hide behind. She breathed deeply.

*Okay Lord. It's not personal. It's not personal. She's really the one that's hiding Lord. I don't have to hide...help her Lord. Help her.*

Christina gathered her courage again, and turned to the next cubicle. Another woman sat in this chair. She watched Christina approach.

"Hi. I'm Christina. I'm a massage therapist and I was just wondering if you would like a complementary massage."

"You're new," the woman said, a slightly mischievous curl to her lips.

"Yes, I am," Christina said, relaxing a little. "You've had massage before I take it."

"Love it," the woman said, settling back for the treat. Her head nestled into her pillow, the movement slightly disrupting the blonde wig on her head. She had a pretty face. She looked to be about the age of Christina's mother.

"Well, good. What's your name and I'll just get out your paperwork."

"Hastings. Jennifer."

Christina went to grab the notebook. Recurring breast cancer. Aggressive. In her third month of chemo. "What do you like when you have massages?" she asked when she returned.

"Everything," Jennifer said, closing her eyes.

Christina's eyes followed the plastic lines tracing through the air next to the bed and disappearing in between two buttons on Jennifer's blouse. Jennifer must have a port, a quarter-sized disc underneath the skin just below her shoulder, into which the needle sticks for the administration of the drugs. "Do you have any new developments I should know about before I start?"

"Not unless you count the engagement of my daughter as a new development."

"Oh!" Christina exclaimed. "Well, it's not important for the massage, but it certainly is an important new development for you! That's exciting!"

"Yes it is. And about time too."

Christina stepped behind the woman and slowly, gently placed her hands on her shoulders. Jennifer kept talking as Christina pressed down and out along the line of her shoulders.

"She's been with this guy for like five years. I kept saying to her, I'd say, 'I really want to go to your wedding. Would you just get married already before it's too late?' I guess they've finally listened to me."

Christina chuckled. "When's the wedding?"

"They're thinking sometime next summer. Hopefully early summer if you know what I mean."

"Hmmm," Christina said.

"My son's already married and, of course I've been begging him and his wife to have a baby already, you know. I don't have any grandkids yet, but, oh man, just to be able to hold a grandbaby before I go...I can't think of anything better...well, seeing my baby girl walk down the aisle...that too."

Christina listened as Jennifer talked. She focused on making her strokes and pressure soft, not too deep; relaxing, not toxin releasing.

Jennifer sat, her eyes closed most of the time, her mouth continuously spilling her heart.

Christina listened and prayed over the woman.

After thirty minutes Jennifer gave a deep sigh. "That was nice. Thank you." She opened her eyes. "I like you. You're a good listener."

"Thank you."

"I hope I get to see you again in here."

"Well, I'll be here every Tuesday afternoon for the next several months. So, if that's when you make your visits, we'll be seeing each other."

"I'll do my best to come on Tuesday afternoons then." Jennifer smiled widely, then closed her eyes and lay back against her pillow.

Christina quietly walked away, feeling very pleased.

She moved along the carpeted room to the next cubicle. Her feet crossed over the boundary line onto white linoleum as she approached the cushioned chair where a middle-aged man sat. His face was a template of tension. His eyes were squeezed shut. Next to him was a woman, heavily burdened with sorrow.

Christina walked softly up to them. Quietly, she said, "Hello."

The man and his wife both looked at her as if she were going to rob them. What they saw was a young girl full of vitality, health and consideration. The fear in their eyes abated slightly.

"I'm Christina and I was wondering if you would like to have a complementary massage."

The man looked confused. "Free massage?"

His wife was looking at him hopefully.

"Yeah," Christina said.

"Is that allowed for cancer patients?"

Christina smiled. "Yes. There are limits of course. But massage done properly is perfectly okay, even good for oncology patients."

The man glanced at his wife, then back at Christina. "Sure, why not," he said with resignation.

"Great. I take it you haven't had one before?"

The man had laid his head back again, his eyes squeezed shut. His wife looked at Christina and shook her head.

"What's your name?" Christina asked.

"Hubert. Jonathan."

In the notebook, she found his file. Metastatic melanoma.

"Anything going on today that I should know about?"

The man huffed through his nose, his mouth sneering. "Nothing new. Everything's just as awful as it's always been."

His wife bowed her head, her hands working knots into her skirt.

Christina sighed and said a quick prayer.

"Would you like me to work your shoulders and head a little bit today?"

"Whatever."

Christina slipped behind the man. His hair was full, if a little brittle. She gently placed her palms onto his shoulders, pressing with minimal pressure down his arms. The man sat quietly. His wife just watched, her lips seeming to tremble every so often.

Their cubicle was heavy with silence. Occasional beeps would sound from other areas when another patient's medicine bag had run empty. Nurses would ruffle by. One peeked in on Jonathan but, seeing Christina at work, moved on.

For fifteen minutes Christina gently rubbed his shoulders and arms. She could feel his muscles relaxing more with each pass of her hands. The lines of his eyes were turning from two tense asterisks to a pair of peaceful dashes. She ran her fingertips up into his hair, letting them travel in large circles along his scalp where his head was not pressed back against the chair. After several minutes, the man's breathing became audible…deep, rolling breaths, in and out with perfect cadence.

A whimper to Christina's left startled her. Jonathan's wife was sobbing quietly, her hand coming to her mouth, her eyes sending big drops down her cheeks.

Christina removed her hands from the man quickly, uncertain if she had done something wrong.

"Is everything okay?"

Through trembling lips, the woman whispered, "He's asleep."

Christina's hands came down to her side, her blood pressure returning to normal. "Oh, well that's a good thing, right?" she quietly asked.

The woman was shaking her head, her eyes still pouring forth, her hand still at her mouth. "He hasn't been able to really relax and sleep for several days now…not since…" she looked around the room, "…all this started."

"Ohhhh," Christina said with understanding. "I'm so sorry about that." She looked at Jonathan. The skin on his face seemed to rest limply against the bones underneath. His parted lips offered no resistance to the in and out of his breathing. His eyelids were perfectly still, covering a dreamless sleep.

"Don't be sorry," the woman said, also watching him sleep. Then she looked up at Christina with wet brown eyes, her breath shaky. "Thank you. Thank you so much."

Christina put a hand on the woman's shoulder.

This was it. She knew what she wanted to do with the rest of her life.

· · · · · · · · ·

"It's really hard. I love it, but it's really hard. I have to set aside my entire day for those visits to the hospital."

Christina was in PA for a visit. She sat on her parent's sofa, her mom and dad each in a chair opposite her.

Her dad nodded understandingly. Her mom watched her.

"I have to emotionally and mentally prepare for it. And then I go do it. And then I have to emotionally and mentally unwind after it." Christina ran her hand through her full head of hair. "But…I really do love it. It seems so perfect for my life, ya know. I wish I could do more of it."

"You can volunteer more time, can't you?" Doug asked.

"Yes... I can always volunteer more time," Christina said. "And once the internship's over, I plan on staying on as a volunteer. It's just hard to imagine giving more time at the hospital when I still need to be trying to make money, and all that nonsense."

JoDee continued to watch her daughter, her eyes squinting in thought.

"I don't know. It's all so confusing: finding something that I really, really love doing, but there's no money in it.

"Christina," JoDee blurted, "you could start a non-profit."

Christina whipped her head forward. "What?!"

"Raise money to support yourself, so that you can do oncology massage full time."

"What?!"

Doug was nodding his head. "It's not a bad idea."

"What are you guys talking about? I could never start a non-profit. I don't even know anything about that kind of stuff."

"Well, people around you could help get it off the ground, if you wanted to do it."

Christina leaned back against the couch cushions and stared at the ceiling.

"It's just a possibility... so you could do oncology massage full time," JoDee said.

"I don't know that I *could* do oncology massage full time," Christina said, shaking her head, her fears and insecurities all she could see on the ceiling. "It's so exhausting. It's hard enough doing it one day a week. How could I ever do it five days a week?" Her mind floated to the many memories in the past month of being turned down on the infusion floor. There had even been a few horrendous afternoons where not a single patient had wanted a massage, and Christina had spent most of her time wandering the floor feeling worthless.

"I just don't know."

Doug shrugged his shoulders. "You should just do what you can."

JoDee shrugged her shoulders too.

They dropped it.

. . . . . . . . .

About a month later, Christina and Linsey sat across from each other catching up and sharing life over a meal at The Melting Pot, just like old times.

"So how's the oncology massage going?"

"It's great!" Christina said enthusiastically. "It really is. It's getting easier to approach the patients. Of course, it helps a lot when there are a bunch of people there that I already know." She pushed some noodles around on her plate. "Some have even told me they try to schedule their appointments around the times when they know I'll be there."

"Of course they do," Linsey said with a wink.

"And it's not so draining to me any more. In fact, in some ways it energizes me. I mean, I still have to set aside the whole day to prep, and unwind and stuff, but it's really something that I look forward to now."

"That's awesome." Linsey pushed her plate aside, wiping her face and settling back into her chair. "It's really cool that you found this program."

"I know. I kind of wish I could do it more often, you know." Christina looked up at Linsey, wondering if she should share her latest thought.

Linsey nodded. "You could volunteer more."

"I know," Christina said, also pushing her plate to the side.

Their waitress came by and dropped off their check. Linsey quickly grabbed it.

"Linsey!"

"Christina! I asked you out to dinner. It's my treat. End of discussion."

Christina shook her head, but expressed her thanks.

"Look, it says here that if we add on an extra 10% to our check, the restaurant will match it and give all of it to the March of Dimes. Maybe I should do that." Linsey was reading from a flyer she had swiped off the edge of their table. "Hmmm. That's a cool way to get donations."

Christina watched Linsey study the charity's flyer. Then she cleared her throat. "Did I tell you my mom suggested a while back that I start a non-profit?"

Linsey's head snapped up. "Huh?"

"That would support me so I could do oncology massage full time."

Linsey's mouth dropped open. "Teena, I love it!"

"You do?" Christina chuckled, surprised at herself that she might have expected Linsey to react any other way.

"Yes! That's awesome!"

"Yeah, it is. I wasn't sure about the idea before, but, I'm starting to think that it might not be a bad idea after all. You know, I wasn't sure that I could do it full time, but it's really become a positive thing for me. I'm beginning to think it might really be something that I *could* do full time."

"Of course you could."

"It's just all that non-profit mumbo-jumbo stuff that I REALLY don't think I could do."

"Oh Christina. I could help you. Oh please, please, please! Oh, I could design a logo for you, make flyers for you, I could set up a marketing strategy, I could solicit donations for you."

Christina chuckled. Linsey listed off all the things Christina feared doing herself, removing in a single conversation the burden from her shoulders. And she knew immediately that the process had begun, and there would be no looking back.

· · · · · · · · ·

"Christina, we got a name! We got a name Christina!"

Christina held her cell back from her ear to wait for Linsey's jubilant, loud words to subside. "Okay…tell me."

"Consider the Sparrow. From Luke 12:6-7 'Are not five sparrows sold for a penny? Yet not one of them is forgotten by God. Indeed, the very hairs of your head are all numbered. Don't be afraid; you are worth more than many sparrows.'."

*Oh Lord.* "I absolutely love it Linsey!" Now Christina's words were jubilant.

"I thought you would."

"I'll tell the board."

The board had formed virtually overnight. Once Christina had told her mom that she was interested in moving forward with the non-profit, a board had been put together consisting of JoDee, Linsey, Tammy Hansen, Leah Tuttle (Linsey's mom), and Nancy Stack. There was a plethora of business and non-profit experience in that group, and Christina was adequately relieved of any duties for

208

the organization other than the actual massage work.

The next step would be raising money.

•  •  •  •  •  •  •  •  •

"Thank you all for being here. I really appreciate everyone who is here. To have people show up to a benefit dinner on a Friday night when you could do more fun things with your life is exciting.

"So, yeah, this vision for Consider the Sparrow has come about in a fun way, a unique way... only God could have done it. I had been working at OHSU for my internship and was probably telling my family stories about all the wonderful people I was meeting, and I began to think 'I wish I would do this forever, for free'...you know... 'if money didn't have to exist I would just do this forever.' Through different conversations with Mom and Dad, Linsey and friends, we began to process what it would look like to start a non-profit where people could donate to a fund that would allow me to do this full time in multiple settings and offer free massage as a straight-up free gift with no strings attached. Those three hours a week at the hospital became the highlight of my week. What if I could do that in multiple hospitals, cancer clinics, hospice care, maybe even in-home hospice care. I just can't think of anything better to be doing with my time.

"There's something so powerful about physically touching somebody... it's indescribable...especially in the cancer world, or the hospital world where touch is so often associated with pain, with someone else giving you another injection or a test. This is a way to reconnect with your body in a sense...to realize your body is not your enemy. It's really neat to offer somebody a massage that can assist in their healing... allows somebody to see something good in their body. I love ministering to family and friends of the patients just as much. They go through the journey with us. Sometimes it feels like their journeys are much harder than our own; they feel out of control, they feel powerless. Sometimes I can bring my story into these situations... of pondering an early death and what that would do to my family. I have plenty of fears of what it would look like for me to face death, what it would look like to watch my family watch me die."

Tears. Sniffs. Smiles.

"But the cool part about that is, that God is enough. If I believe him to be enough for me, then he's enough for my family. It's even cool that it's such a tender subject for me, because that translates when I'm talking to my patients about it. And my fears are just as real as theirs. But my hope is real too. And my hope doesn't go away, and my joy doesn't go away. That joy God gives, and the peace God gives is the biggest gift I could ever imagine. And being able to work in this field with people walking that same journey, it's a privilege to be able to share with them. Whether or not they're believers people always ask how you get through, and all I can do is share what He's done for me and how I walk through my own journey, which is through God. There's an avenue there that wouldn't exist without my story. This isn't something that I would change...because I wouldn't trade that avenue for anything. It's a very tender place to enter with somebody, but there's this unspoken permission that happens when you share that trial... they let you in quicker, and you can go there. That's where the excitement comes for me in this whole field. That's where I get elated. I get energy from being in that situation. It takes a toll too...but in the end I always go home with energy. It's always amazing.

"It's a place that I feel absolutely led. I'll always have struggles, I'll always have fears, but I know my God is enough. God just tells me over and over again, 'I just want you to walk in faith.' I don't want to stand in the way of anything He wants to do. If He wants to use my story to encourage people walking my same journey, I couldn't be more excited.

"We're just holding the dreams loosely, knowing that God could do anything. The dreams are really open and it could look like a lot of things. I know that my diagnosis could change on a dime. It could be done like that. But I'm alive today, and today I'm excited about this dream. I have no idea what He wants to do with it but it's exciting to have you guys a part of it. Thank you all for being here and letting me speak. I feel super inadequate and I always fight those feelings, but God is teaching me a lot about that. I'm just thankful for all you guys' support and thankful for life and every minute that I get to be alive and feel healthy. And even if I don't feel healthy I'm still alive and I'm still able to share and be a witness for Him."

· · · · · · · · ·

Christina pulled her car into the parking lot at OHSU. It had been a couple weeks since the benefit dinner and though she hadn't heard any solid numbers, she had been told by the board that the fundraiser had gone well. A meeting was in the works between Christina and Tammy Hanson to go over the hours and expectations of the charity.

Christina turned the engine off but left the worship song on. She sang along, praising God for where He had brought her. She was right where she wanted to be.

Her phone rang. She turned down the song and answered it. "Don't!"

"You don't!" Linsey answered.

"How are you?"

"Gettin' huger by the minute! This baby's gonna to be a moose if he keeps growing at this rate."

"It just means you're doing well by him, keeping him well fed and all secure in there."

"Yeah, I guess so. Hey, I wanted to tell you: 'Consider the Sparrow' got a phone call today."

"Really?" Christina found herself smiling widely with surprise.

"Yeah, and it was really cool Christina. This woman, her name was Olga, had found us on the Internet...and when I started telling her about us, she just kept saying, 'Is it true?' And I'm like 'Is what true?' She goes, 'Do you really give free massages for people with cancer?' I'm like, 'Oh, yeah. It's totally true. That's what we do.' She was so overwhelmed with gratitude, she almost couldn't speak. It was really cute."

"Wow. That is so cool."

"She's in her second round of treatments. She lives alone in McMinnville."

"Wow."

"She is the lost and forgotten Christina."

"You're right. She is."

"But no one is forgotten, eh?"

"No one is forgotten. Thanks for letting me know."

"Yeah. I told her you would be calling her."

"Thanks Linsey. That's great."

"'Is it true?'"

"It's true."

• • • • • • • • •

Christina walked onto the infusion floor, scanning the room for familiar faces. She smiled as a couple patients called to her.

"Christina!"

"Hey Billy. Nice to see you. Hi Patricia!"

She checked in, grabbed her folder and walked toward the corner cubicle. Laura, a grandmotherly figure with a flowery green bandanna wrapped around her head, was there alone. Her thin body seemed to melt into the leather chair.

"Christina," she said through a cracking smile, her voice as broken as her body.

"Hi Laura. How are you feeling today?"

"Oh...I'm here."

"You are here. And you look great."

Laura waved a wiry hand off the bed, a sheet of blue veins and wrinkles over bone. "Now you're just lying."

"No, I'm not Laura. I think you *do* look great."

Laura smiled with a slight turn of her head. On the table next to her bed a cup of orange juice sat untouched, a straw slanting toward Laura's uninterested face.

"Anything new I should know about?"

"Nope."

Christina placed a hand on Laura's foot.

Laura smiled. Her eyes frequently closed into long blinks, always ending in a strained lifting of her eyelids to reveal that Laura's eyes had stayed trained on Christina.

"Should we do some feet today?"

"Yes, please."

Christina settled at the foot of the bed.

The room seemed warmer than normal today. She could feel a stickiness forming under the hairs that lay against her neck. She quickly tossed her hair back to let the open air dry her skin. A blue heated blanket covered the woman, from the two lumps that were her feet, to the empty pocket where her chest met her chin. The only parts of Laura other than her head, that braved exposure were her two arms; her right resting motionless atop the blanket, strewn across her belly like a neglected appendage; her left set against the armrest, the crease in the elbow open and punctured as the port into her body. Carefully, Christina grabbed the corner of the cloth and folded it back up to Laura's knees, a smile cracking her face as she did so. On Laura's feet was a pair of bright pink socks with multicolored butterflies dancing a Mayday dance around her pole ankles.

"Butterflies today, huh?"

Laura's lips stretched quickly into a smile. "I saw my first butterfly of the year yesterday."

Christina smiled.

She gently placed her hands on Laura's left foot. It was bony, hard, used. And it was cold... deeply chilled, as if its distance from the source of heat in Laura's body had, over time, left it more and more isolated, forgotten. Christina felt a choke forming in her throat. She swallowed hard. A brief glance upward revealed that Laura was still looking at her. Quickly, Christina flashed her a loving smile. Laura returned it.

Christina softly squeezed Laura's foot to acclimate her to the warm touch. Then, she carefully pressed her thumbs up the arches, from the heel's callous, to the balls' callous; from one end of Laura's life to the other, touching all her wounded and hurting places, reminding Laura of her loveliness.

*Lord, help Laura today. Help her relax. Help her remember that she is fearfully and wonderfully made. Help her know that she is not forgotten.*

Christina noticed that Laura's foot in her hand was small, fragile, bony, too easily broken...what she imagined the foot of a bird might feel like.

Rather...like a sparrow's.

*So where does that leave us today? Well...ALIVE for one thing!!! Yaaaaayyyy! It is so GOOD to be alive. You are alive and I am alive...today, right now, this moment. From those of you 'healthy as a horse' types, to those of you hanging on by your fingernails...today, we share together. We are alive! Do you appreciate that today? It definitely wasn't something I appreciated on a regular basis until, well I was told I might not have as many years as I've always pictured. So I know I have a little advantage over some of you in terms of being 'forced' into this mindset, but hey, regardless of how difficult or easy your circumstances are today...do you appreciate the significance of how exciting it is that you get to be alive today? Wooooo!!!!!*

*I'd like to leave you with a passage on my heart today from Psalm 27:*

> *"The Lord is my light and salvation;*
>    *of whom shall I be afraid?*
> *When evil men advance against me*
>    *to devour my flesh...my heart will not fear;*
> *Though war break out against me,*
>    *even then will I be confident.*
>
> *Teach me Your way, O Lord;*
>    *lead me in a straight path*
>    *because of my oppressors.*
>
> *I am still confident of this;*
>    *I will see the goodness of the Lord*
>    *in the land of the living.*
> *Wait for the Lord;*
>    *be strong and take heart*
>  *and wait for the Lord."*

*Love,*

*Christina*

By faith, Christina persevered as one who knew that the Lord was enough for her.

"Therefore, since we are surrounded by such a great cloud of witnesses, let us throw off everything that hinders and the sin that so easily entangles, and let us run with perseverance the race marked out for us."

Hebrews 12:1

# And Now?

Christina had a recurrence in fall of 2010. After another surgery and a round of chemotherapy, her journey continues.

She has continued her pursuit of oncology massage with more intensive training with hospital patients on the cancer floors at Oregon Health and Sciences University. After her latest round of surgery and treatment, Christina's passion for oncology massage has increased. She continues to work under her non-profit, Consider the Sparrow, and still hopes to be God's instrument for the 'lost and forgotten.'

PS: She just got married!! (11/26/11)

For more information on Christina, and for updates, visit:
www.christinaahmann.com

For more information on Consider the Sparrow, visit:
www.considerthesparrow.org

This song was written by Christina's friend Andrea Davenport. It is available on iTunes, with all proceeds going to Consider the Sparrow.

<u>You Consider Me</u>
By Andrea Davenport


I've never walked this way before
These steps are new, the path unsure
You know this much, You wrote my name
You consider me.

There's joy in what I cannot see
Surely this was meant for me
You consider me.

An old life stripped away
Leaving familiar to yesterday
I'm pursuing You recklessly
Abandon it all, confidently.

Fear has no place in me
Your strength secures its bold defeat
Refining fire alive in me
You consider me.

These timid feet, they are mine no more
I will boldly go, I will stand before
I'll sing aloud, unashamed
I'll declare this now and bless Your name.

There's joy in what I cannot see
You consider me.

# Note from the Author

In the fall of 1996, as a senior in high school, I walked into the sixth period freshman orchestra class to offer my services in the guiding of our school's future symphonic orchestra. Amongst the young violinists sat a petite 14-year-old girl with short brown hair, a VERY quiet disposition, and a winning smile. I had seen her before, at church and through my association with her brother Jesse. I may have spoken briefly with her...but I'm quite sure that, apart from shy smiles and practically imperceptible nods, she never spoke a word to me. After a year of walks between classes, hanging out on her trampoline, and chats over cappuccino blasts, she finally believed that I enjoyed her company and wanted to be her friend.

Fifteen years later, Christina and I are still friends, despite the obstacles of distance, time and my three children.

A year and a half ago, through various nudges, I was compelled to offer my help in spreading Christina's story to more hearts ready to hear it. I cried over my keyboard as I lived through my dear friend's struggles. But through it all, her story ultimately pointed me, as I hope it does for you, to the loving care of our sovereign God.